SOME SOURCES OF SOUTHERNISMS

SOME SOURCES OF

Southernisms

By M. M. MATHEWS

1948

University of Alabama Press

UNIVERSITY, ALABAMA

Foreword

SOME SOURCES OF SOUTHERNISMS is the fourth of the Dancy Series of Lectures to be delivered at Alabama College, an event of April 24 and 25, 1947. These lectures are now ready for the reading public as the Dancy Endowment prescribes.

Alabama College made a felicitous choice, as the reader will discover, in selecting Dr. Mathews, an eminent lexicographer and native Alabamian, to deliver the 1947 Dancy Lectures.

ELLEN-HAVEN GOULD,
Chairman Faculty Committee on the Dancy Lectures.

Alabama College, Montevallo, Alabama
December, 1947

Preface

*T*HE THREE ESSENTIAL parts of this book were delivered at Alabama College for Women at Montevallo, April 24-5, 1947, as the fourth series of the Dancy Lectures. I have availed myself of the publisher's kind invitation to present here a somewhat fuller version of the lectures than was given at Montevallo. It is to be hoped, however, that no one will get the impression that the subjects dealt with in the following pages are anything like exhaustively treated even in this expanded form.

Southernisms, that is, those words and meanings of words that came first into use in the South, have never been thoroughly studied. The larger subject of Americanisms in general has not so far awakened the interest it deserves and that, in time, it will surely receive.

The linguistic scene presented here in the United States is unique in the history of civilization, though as yet there has not been anything like general realization of this fact. Never before has such uniformity of speech as we are accustomed to in this country prevailed over an area of some three million square miles and extending through about twenty-five degrees of latitude and fifty degrees of longitude. The

135,000,000 people inhabiting this great country are not separated by a single linguistic barrier. We have among us representatives or descendants of a great number of the so-called 'races' of the earth, but with negligible variations we all use the same speech.

What the ultimate significance of such linguistic unity is to be, no man can say. The fact is easily observable, however, that students all over the world are more and more directing their attention to American English as their second language. This preference for our variety of English is especially observable here in the Western Hemisphere. Mario A. Pei, a competent scholar, estimates that we have in the New World at least 145,000,000 people who use the English language. Spanish with its 83,000,000 is the nearest competing language, with Portuguese, 44,000,000, coming third. More people influential in world affairs can be reached by English than by any other language. English is not going to become a world language; it is already that. And it is the American variety of English that is predominating.

In view of this situation, it is particularly fitting that those of us who use American English should make a serious and sustained effort to find out all we can about it. In the following pages the nature of what may be discovered is indicated in a way, I trust, to stimulate other and better scholars to more extensive and intensive work in this most interesting field.   .

At any rate, the information here set forth, despite the pioneer nature of the undertaking, will, I hope, be of somewhat general interest, and especially so to at least a few of those who are glad to take their "stand, and live and die in Dixie."

M. M. MATHEWS

University of Chicago Press
July, 1947

Contents

1 · The Nahuatl Contribution to Southern Speech

At THE OUTSET of these lectures there are some general observations that should be made in an effort to make clear the nature and scope of what is here undertaken.

Although a great many people, among them some who are highly intelligent and well educated, never heard of such a thing, there are in everyday use among us hundreds and even thousands of words that either originated in this country or that have here taken on meanings they never had in the speech of Great Britain. Such a statement as this justifies us in pausing, in order for this idea to sink well into the minds of all present.

Formal education inevitably and properly leads people into the remote past. To begin at the beginning is an old and wise procedure, but from following it there often result attitudes that hinder a person from becoming satisfactorily oriented with reference to the everyday world in which he, perforce, must live. The proneness of scholars to live and move and have their intellectual being in times long gone by and in places away from where men congregate accounts, in large measure, for the ridicule sometimes heaped upon them, and for the cartoons representing them as funny old fuss-budgets without much practical sense. This attitude toward learned gentlemen is also reflected in such expressions as 'absentminded professor' and 'brain-trusters.'

Perhaps those scholars who devote their lives to the study of language are especially in danger of getting out of touch with the things of everyday life. In plowing through the ruins of old civilizations and in puzzling over badly weathered inscriptions made before the dawn of historic times, they may lose their perspective. We of course owe a debt of gratitude to those heroic souls who have in many instances returned to us from their far wanderings with their minds richly fraught with fascinating cargoes from long silent places. They have helped us to understand the past, and by so doing they have helped us to understand ourselves.

But by no means all of the young mariners who sail away into and beyond the rosy dawn of history's beginnings are fortunate in their tremendous labors and vexations of head and heart wherein they labor under the sun in those far-off climes. Often they come home with empty hands, and with dazed brains surcharged with speculations of what might have been. Sometimes they are able to unload these cargoes of imagination all compact into learned disquisitions that appear in published form in the proceedings of societies of ancient and honorable repute. Sometimes, in the white winter of their old age, they get rid of an entire book-load of clever hypotheses that have long been their stock in trade before many a class of bored students weary with incomprehension.

Such scholarly journeyers into the wastelands of long past times often fail to notice the linguistic phenomena that are all about them. The lure of the long ago and far away often greatly exceeds that which is exercised by the near at hand and ever present. It was not until he was old and ready to die that the old man in the fable who lived at the bottom of the sea discovered water.

Fortunately nowadays increasingly large numbers of energetic young students are giving enthusiastic attention to the linguistic phenomena in the very midst of which they have fortunately been placed. They are becoming increasingly aware of the richness of the field of American English for studies of divers kinds. They are making valuable discoveries, and are deepening and broadening their acquaintance with our country's past through a close study of the language which our ancestors used.[1]

A great part of the language which we find of

most use was made right here at home. It was evolved
during the course of a civilization which is unique in
the annals of history. There is a tendency sometimes
observable on the part of those unacquainted with the
contributions made in this country to the resources of
the English language to belittle our achievements in
this realm of culture. It is a strange and often commented upon trait of human nature that we remember people by the bad things they have done, and yet
flatter ourselves that we will be remembered by our
admirable achievements. If the Apostle Peter should
return to this earth he would no doubt be grieved to
find that very few people are acquainted with his
marvelous speech on Mars Hill, but everybody is
quite familiar with the denial episode.

Proceeding in accordance with this trait of our
character, we quite easily recognize and bear in mind
the unworthy contributions made to the English language in this country. Surely most people would
recognize our slang expression, *to chew the rag,* as
an Americanism, but the number who recognizes *rag
carpet* and *rag rug* as American contributions to the
language is probably small. *To euchre* in the sense
of to cheat or deceive is easily recognizable as an
American contribution, but *euchre* as the name of a
card game escapes detection. Our lexicographers
often innocently foster this trend of recognizing the

bad and remaining unaware of the good in our linguistic contributions. *Buck* meaning a dollar is dutifully recorded as being of United States provenience, but under *appendicitis* compensatory information to the effect that this word is an American contribution to the language is omitted.

This whole tendency to regard words made in the United States as unworthy and those brought in from abroad as of honorable station, is common, but it is entirely in error. Just as the language of an individual is an index of his culture and of his past, so the language prevailing in a great nation such as ours is an index of its culture and of its past. If the additions we have made to the English language are contemptible ones, rest assured that the culture out of which this contribution evolved is likewise contemptible. The language which we have made is an indication of our accomplishments in the hundreds of directions in which we have enlightened the world. The relationship observed in ancient times between a tree and its fruit holds true when there is considered a nation's accomplishments and a nation's means of expression.

Every American is confronted daily with such a bewilderingly large number of things peculiar to his civilization that he pays little attention to any of them, taking them for granted, as it is quite natural for him to do. It simply never occurs to him that such terms as *automobile, rocking chair, wash-rag, carpet sweeper, radio, chewing gum, refrigerator, radiator, ice box, dresser, cook-book, egg-beater, waffle iron, wash-board, dish pan, dish rag, wash pan, harmonica, phonograph, appendicitis, demoralize, belittle, lengthy, overalls, overcoat, shirt waist, cafeteria, delicatessen, campus, fraternity, sorority, co-ed, congressional, ice pick, sleigh, toboggan, hickory, pecan,* and thousands of others, in the senses in which we use them, originated right here in our country, and are well worth the serious study of all who are interested in understanding the background out of which our present has developed.

A good understanding of the circumstances under which each word we have first used made its appearance is well worth much effort to obtain. There is a reason why *hydrant* originated in this country, and why Philadelphia was the city where it first came into use. There is a reason for the appearance first in this country of 'hip pockets' in trousers, and a further reason why such convenient receptacles are reported first from the South. The most commonplace of our contributions have much to teach us. There is a reason why 'boiled shirts' were never spoken of until gold was discovered in California. *Plug hat* could not have made its appearance among us before 1807 or thereabouts, and in fact it came in much later than that. There is an obvious reason why *juke box* was first used in this country, and why the South was the birthplace of it.

By this time you are no doubt quite reconciled to the idea, which may have appeared novel to you at first, that a great many words and a great many new meanings of words have arisen in this country. It will no doubt be easy for you to advance one step further in getting in harmony with the spirit of these lectures and realize that a great many words have come first into use in the English language here in the South. Not a few of the words that were first taken over into the language in this part of the country have now become well known elsewhere, but we shall not place any emphasis on that aspect of the matter. The important thing for us just now is to bear in mind that in this series of lectures our primary object is to examine the sources of some of these words that have been added to our vocabulary here in the South. The designation Southernisms will be used for terms of this kind.

Having thus explained the general nature of our interest, we now proceed to a second aspect of our undertaking. In this lecture, and in the one which follows it, we shall devote some attention to Indian words that have become part of our Southern vocabulary. Before beginning an enumeration of such words as these, it will be helpful for us to pay some attention to the Indians themselves and to their languages. We can of course not afford to devote much time to this phase of our subject, but to ignore it completely might encourage the delusion that language exists in a vacuum, and that those who speak it are of no interest. The fact is of course that the study of language should go hand in hand with the study of history, ethnology, anthropology, and all other subjects having to do with man in his manifold relationships.

When we were small we learned that Columbus discovered America in 1492. As we grew older some of us found that our country had certainly been discovered by Norsemen centuries before Columbus was born. As we continued to learn, we made the acquaintance of books written to show that for generations before Columbus sailed westward there were many Portuguese navigators who not only knew that there was land in the far west, but had themselves sailed thither.[2] And then, finally, we learned that some ten or fifteen thousand years before Columbus, America had not only been discovered but also settled by Asiatic peoples who before the dawn of history began trekking across from Siberia by way of Bering Strait and settling or roving in all parts of

North and South America. Without a doubt poor old
Columbus is to be regarded as a Johnny-come-lately,
and the lateness of his coming is to be measured in
thousands of years rather than in centuries.

Despite much prolonged study and investigation
of the subject, very little is actually known about the
origin of the American Indians. The view now current among anthropologists is that the Indians found
here by Europeans in the fifteenth and following
centuries were the descendants of Asiatic migrants
representing a composite of several strains, the most
important of which was Mongoloid. There is a tendency on the part of those of us without instruction in
the matter to think of all the American Indians as
belonging to the same type, and as manifesting uni-
form physical characteristics. The fact is that there
were so many different types of Indians that scholars have been driven to conclude that their ancestors
must have come from various peoples of northern,
central, and eastern Asia.

It is perhaps hardly necessary to mention that this
view of the origin of the Indians, and of the way
they entered this country, is not one which is ac-
cepted by all scholars. The views on the subject have
been numerous and varied, and even yet there is no
perfect agreement on the matter. But the sentiment
expressed is the most prevalent one at present.[3]

The ultimate origin of the Indians, no matter how intriguing a subject it may be in and for itself, is of only secondary interest in our present undertaking, so we may pass on to some consideration of the language situation as it existed among them. And here we come upon a state of affairs quite as puzzling and baffling as the question of the origin of the Indians in the first place.

Those who have never had occasion to look into the matter may well be surprised to learn that there was no one Indian language that prevailed over practically this entire country. We have at present only one prevailing form of speech throughout the United States. Might it not have been the same with the Indians who formerly occupied this area?

Scholars tell us that if we count both North and South America, the number of separate and distinct Indian languages or language stocks or language families known to have been in use by the natives is no less than about 160. These different languages were split up into dialects, and in the total of some 160 languages there existed about 1200 of these dialectal subdivisions. In what is now Canada and the United States there were, according to the best estimates scholars can make, Indians speaking about six hundred dialects. A conservative guess as to the number of Indian tribes in this same region places them at 1200. If 1200 tribes spoke 600 dialects it does not take much of a mathematician to see that, on the average, there was a dialect for every two tribes. Some of these dialects were mutually intelligible but many of them were not, for they represented at least fifty or sixty different languages, and these languages differed far more than do modern English and modern German.

The language situation as it existed among the Indians in this country has caused scholars to study and philosophize at great length. The most bewildering fact about this entire matter is that so far as can be learned there is no indication that the 160 or so Indian languages in North and South America were in any way related. Scholars found out long ago that while English and German and Dutch are now mutually unintelligible, they all three are quite closely related. They have a common ancestry. Similarly, languages such as French, Spanish, Portuguese, and Italian, are closely related, all of them stemming from vulgar Latin in fairly recent times. All efforts to relate the Indian languages and so derive them from a prehistoric common source have failed. Nor has there been any success whatever attained in trying to relate any of the American Indian languages to any form of expression now used in Asia. If the ancestors of the Indians came from various parts of Asia, one would certainly expect to find some linguistic traces of the former identity of the peoples, but not a vestige of resemblance of this kind has been found.[4]

Fortunately for us, we are not here called upon to puzzle our heads about this tremendous problem. With the preceding remarks to serve as a background, we may proceed now to a discussion of the Nahuatl language, the source of numerous words that have filtered into English usage.

The Nahua were the most important of the races found by the Spaniards in what is now Mexico in the sixteenth century. They occupied the plateau region extending from the Rio Grande to Guatemala. The date of their arrival in that region is not known, but fortunately does not concern us here. It is of more importance for us to know that their descendants to the number of nearly two million are still living in that same general area, the Mexican native Indians today belonging in the main to this ancient stock. The Aztecs were the most important of the Nahua people, and sometimes the term Aztec is applied to all the Nahua tribes in Mexico at the time of the Spanish conquest. Nahuatl is the name given to the language spoken by the Aztecs, and it also designates the closely related dialects which taken together constitute the Nahuatlan branch of what is known as the Uto-Aztecan linguistic family, one of the most important and widespread of the American Indian families of language.[5]

Some of the Nahua Indians had made greater cultural progress than had any other of the American Indian peoples. Of particular interest to us here is the fact that they had developed the art of making paper,[6] and had a system of writing. Unfortunately for students of their language, the Nahuas had advanced no further in their writing than to the stage of using pictographs. They had carried this type of writing to such a degree of perfection, however, that some scholars are convinced that had it not been for the Spanish conquest, these Indians would have discovered all over again the art of writing in the sense in which we are familiar with the term.[7]

When the Spaniards under Cortez began the conquest of Mexico in 1519 there began to percolate into all the languages of Europe, by way of Spanish, a number of words taken from the language of the Nahuatl Indians. English shared in this early linguistic influx, and although some of the words borrowed then lie entirely outside the scope of our investigation it will nevertheless be well enough for us to notice a few of them briefly.

In the forefront of those Nahuatl terms that began to pass into English, by way of Spanish, French, and Portuguese in the sixteenth century, were no doubt many of the place names with which we are familiar today. The dates, even approximately, at which these names became familiar to users of English can not be made out, as there has not been collected any evidence that would enable us to judge how long such terms as *Mexico, Aztec, Nahuatl, Guatemala,* and many others, have been a part of the English vocabulary. In the case of a good many such terms, we are in position to know something of their ultimate signification. *Mexico* preserves the name of an Aztec war god whose domain once embraced the country which is now so named.[8] *Aztec* comes to us from a Nahuatl word meaning 'place of the heron,' or 'heron people.'[9] It alludes to the region from which these Indians came into the area in Mexico where they were when the Spaniards arrived. Where these 'heron people' came from can not be definitely stated. It was somewhere to the northwest, probably, of their Mexican home. *Nahuatl,* so we are told by one whose scholarship is apparently not such as to cause us to place too much reliance in his findings, means 'sweet sounding.'[10] Presumably, with reference to the language it alluded to the melodiousness of the Indians' speech. *Guatemala* is said to be derived from the Aztec word for wood.[11]

There is of course a large number of these Aztec

place names, many of which must have come early into English. All one has to do to become impressed with the multiplicity of these terms is to consult a map of Mexico and consider the many names of places and rivers he finds there. Perhaps most school children, sooner or later, make the acquaintance of the Mexican name *Chapultepec,* and may be interested to find that the significance of it in the parent language is 'grasshopper hill.' In the picture-writing of the Aztecs this place is represented by a drawing of a hill with a grasshopper sitting on top of it. The shape of the hill on which the city was built suggested its name.[12] In this connection it may be of interest to some to know that the volcano, *Popocatepetl,* has a name of Aztec origin, and that it means just what it should, namely, 'smoking mountain.'[13] The term was a great bugbear to me as a youthful student of geography, and I remember with grim satisfaction the pronunciation which my fellow sufferers and I bestowed upon this strange looking name, 'Pop-a-caterpillar.'

Among those words other than proper nouns that came early into English as a result of the conquest of Mexico by the Spaniards, there were some that became so firmly embedded in the language that they have maintained a place of security ever since. One such word is *tomato.* This word made its appearance in English certainly by 1604, in which year one writer described this fruit as "a great sappy and savourie graine"—a statement which reminds us that there was a time in the history of our language when *grain* was used in the sense of a berry, a meaning still preserved in the French word *graine*.[14] For the common words *cocoa* and *chocolate,* we are indebted to Nahuatl.

Others of those words which became a part of the English language in early times were brought once more into our variety of English when, in the early part of the nineteenth century, our pioneering forefathers had pushed their way to what we now know as the Southwest. It is interesting to observe that when Spaniards in the New World became familiar with the pear shaped fruit characteristic of Mexico and the West Indies, they had difficulty in pronouncing the Aztec name of it. The *Oxford English Dictionary* gives the impression that the Spaniards had so much difficulty with this term that it was not long until by popular etymology the Spanish word *avocado* meaning an advocate, was used for the fruit. If this was the state of affairs, it is odd that no Spanish dictionary records *avocado* in this or any other sense, though of course *abogado* is the usual Spanish word for 'lawyer.' The English, from whatever forms of the word they had at their disposal, including such French terms as *aguacat, avocat,* arrived at forms like *avogato, avocato, avigato, avocado,* and finally as if in desperation at *alligator pear*—certainly a far cry from the Nahuatl term, rendered by the first Spaniards to hear it as something like *ahuacatl,* and pronounced the Lord only knows how.

Anyway, *avocado* emerged as a part of the English vocabulary by the latter part of the seventeenth century and has maintained its place ever since. But according to the evidence now available, we in this country made little or no use of this British borrowing. In due time, when our civilization made contact with that of the Spaniards in the Southwest, American pioneers found a welter of Spanish and native forms of this old Nahuatl name. Out of these, and out of such other materials as they might have had at hand, they fashioned afresh the name *avocado.* The suspicion is justified that the currency of this word here in the early nineteenth century owes most if not all its energy to this new taking over of a term that had earlier, by another and entirely different route, made its way into the British usage.

In a similar manner, the well known word *chilli* passed from Nahuatl into Spanish, and in due course from Spanish into English. It arrived in English certainly as early as 1662, and as the name for the dried pods of a species of red pepper it has been cur-

rent ever since. The earliest American evidence for
the use of the term, however, sets in at the time we
began to make first hand acquaintance with the
Spanish speakers on our Southwestern border. The
circumstances make it entirely likely, therefore, that
our use of *chilli* is to be ascribed, not to a continuation on our part of the British tradition, but to the
fact that we borrowed the term from Spanish speakers here in the New World. At any rate, the word
has been of a good deal more importance to us than
it ever was to the British users of it. For example,
we have used it in the sense of a dish or sauce seasoned with chile, and we have spoken of *chile colorado,* that is, red chile, in referring to red pepper, and
we have also used the expression *chile con carne* to
name a dish which one Spanish lexicographer describes as "a detestable food which, with the false
title of Mexican, is sold in the United States from
Texas to New York."[15]

We do not have space here to take up all those
Nahuatl words that have apparently come into the
English language twice—once long ago in Europe
and again more recently in our own Southwest—but
one or two more of them must be included because of
their special interest.

The Spaniards found in Mexico a town the name
of which they wrote down as *Xalapa,* but the modern

form of which is *Jalapa*. In the full form of the
name in Aztec there was an -*n* at the end of it,
Xalapan, but the Spanish in writing those Aztec
names that ended thus dropped the final -*n* if the
names were accented on the penult, the result of this
procedure being that *Guatemala* and *Jalapa* are
names slightly curtailed from what they were in the
Aztec speech. In this town of *Xalapa* the Spaniards
found that the Indians concocted a purgative drug,
and the Spaniards named the drug from the place of
its manufacture, 'purge of Jalapa' (*purga de Jalapa*). This term *jalapa* passed from the Spanish into
French where it became still further curtailed and
was written as *jalap*. From French it passed into
English as our well known word *jalap*.[16]

This account does not quite complete the story,
however. During the Mexican War many volunteers
from all parts of our country went to Mexico, and
there some of them became acquainted at first hand
with this Mexican town of Jalapa. When they returned home from the war the name of the town remained in their minds, and in at least one instance,
so I am informed, led to the naming of a country
town, Jalapa, Indiana. Another returning soldier
went home to Tennessee and there is in that state a
Jalapa, possibly named in similar fashion. A glance
at any good gazetteer will show other places called

Jalapa. It might be difficult to prove that all of them, or even any of them, were named by soldiers returning from the Mexican War, but that theory has been advanced, and on the face of it appears reasonable.[17]

The word *ocelot*, the name of a large leopard-like cat which ranges from Texas into South America, is not only an example of a word borrowed twice into the English language, but is more baffling in its origin than lexicographers have usually pointed out. The word was used by Oliver Goldsmith in 1774 in his work on natural history published in that year. Goldsmith obtained the word from the writings of the celebrated French scientist and author Buffon. The statement is made in dictionaries that Buffon obtained the word *ocelot* by dismembering a Nahuatl word, *tlalocelotl*. This expression is made up of two words, *tlalli* meaning 'field,' and *ocelotl*, 'jaguar.' The Aztec expression therefore upon which Mons. Buffon operated somewhat ruthlessly meant 'field jaguar,' and was the name by which the Aztecs knew the ocelot. But when the Aztecs used the latter part of the name alone, *ocelotl*, they designated the jaguar, the largest and most formidable quadruped of the cat family found in America, being about twice the size of the ocelot.

Dictionaries point out that Buffon by taking the latter portion only of a name the signification of

which he may not have fully appreciated, really gave
the name of the jaguar to the ocelot. This story is
pleasant enough, and the mistake to which it alludes,
if it were really made by Buffon, is certainly a harm-
less one. But there is reason for doubting seriously
that Buffon ever made such an error as has been ascribed to him. Long after Buffon had passed to his
reward, American frontiersmen who had reached
the Southwest used the name *ocelot* for the well
known smaller cat of that region. The question at
once arises as to how they, just as Buffon, picked
up the wrong name for this smaller animal. Had
they read Buffon, or perhaps Goldsmith, and were
they in their accounts of what they had seen using
the same mistaken terminology that Buffon had been
the first to devise? It does not seem at all likely that
the first Americans in the Southwest had heard
much about the nature writings of either of these distinguished men, and yet they used the same name for
the same cat that Buffon had used. The suspicion is
justified that in Nahuatl the word *ocelotl* was employed for just the creature that Goldsmith represented it as being used.[18]

We shall now proceed to take up for consideration
some of those new words that began to pass into
American English in the Southwest as soon as
American frontiersmen came in contact with the

Spaniards in that area. It was, as a rule, through the instrumentality of Spanish that these Nahuatl borrowings were made. The problem of whether we received a word directly from the Indians or indirectly from the Spaniards who had previously taken the word from the natives is interesting but can not well be solved with the evidence now at our disposal. No doubt words from the Aztecs came to us by both the direct and the indirect routes, but we shall not here bother about the particular road over which a word passed in reaching us, being content for the present to regard our Nahuatl terms as coming, usually, by way of Spanish.

We shall also refrain from exhibiting, in a brief treatise such as this, all the words that might properly be placed on display here. So far as I know, there has never been made out a full list of our borrowings from Nahuatl, but a good many of them have been identified, and in the footnotes I shall enumerate a few others at my disposal that, for one reason or another, are not included in the following discussion.[19]

When Europeans came into contact with American Indians, some of their earliest borrowings from the natives were terms denoting foods and drinks. When the Spaniards came into Mexico they observed that the Indians there pounded various seeds into powder or flour for use as food. Parched corn was often pounded up into meal which was then sometimes sweetened and moistened. The food obtained from this powdering process was called by the Indians *pinolli,* and the Spaniards took the thing and the word and passed them on to Americans. Just as no two cooks prepare the same article of food in precisely the same manner, so among the Indians there were different ways of making pinole. Sometimes mesquite-beans, or wheat, was added to the corn, and when the ingredients had been pounded together the resulting flour was moistened to make a thick gruel-like beverage. In this form the food was known to the Indians as *atolli.* This word also came into American English, by way of Spanish, just as *pinolli* did, the Spanish and American English form of the latter word being *atole.* An Indian could no doubt tell quickly which preparation was pinolli and which was atolli, but an examination of the pronouncements of those who have written about these two words leaves the reader with the impression that sometimes there was not much difference between the preparations denoted by them.

The fact that pinole was often the meal or flour obtained from parched corn reminds us that there are those who remember that in their younger days it was customary for children to take those seeds of popcorn that failed to pop, and grind them in the family coffee mill, obtaining thus a meal which when suitably sweetened with sugar and moistened made a preparation that children enjoyed under the name of *cold flour.* There is no doubt but that the ancestors of those children who amused themselves with cold flour had used a similar preparation, similarly named, and consisting of parched corn pounded in a mortar and mixed with one third its quantity of sugar. Our pioneer ancestors carried such cold flour as this with them when they had to go on long journeys. Two or three teaspoonfuls of this sweetened meal when stirred into a glass of water made a most refreshing beverage, and was reputed for its capacity to sustain one in the absence of other food.

No doubt the pioneer frontiersmen who used cold flour learned to do so from the Indians. The Algonquian Indians made use of just such a meal which some of them called by a name which white people wrote as *nocake.* As early as 1634 a writer gave an account of how the New England Indians parched or roasted corn in the ashes, beat it into a powder, and stowed it away for future use. The likelihood is that it was this Indian term *nocake* which lies back of our word *hoe-cake.* At any rate, no better origin for *hoe-cake* can at present be made out. Other New England Indians living only a few miles from those who used the term *nocake* knew the same article of food as *rokehigan,* or *rok'hig.* White people borrowed this term in the form *rokeag.* This meal of powdered parched corn was one of the most widespread foods found among the Indians in North and South America, being used from Canada to Chile. The names which the Europeans found in use for it by various Indian peoples were quite varied. Some of those that have been recorded, in addition to those already given, are *psitamun, nuk'hik, yok'hig, tiste, aparumenan.* It was the principal food of Indian war parties, being so light that an Indian could carry a supply sufficient for a long journey. Under the name of *mashika* it forms an important part of the rations furnished Peruvian soldiers, and the names *mashca* and *machica* are used by the natives in Ecuador for what we know as hominy, a preparation of Indian corn not altogether unlike that denoted by *nocake.*

We have of course wandered some distance away from our Nahuatl words *pinole* and *atole.* We can easily get back to the main body of our subject, however, by remarking that *pinole* which came into American English in the Southwest as early as 1844 is now fairly well known all over the country, but *atole* has not become so generally known. Another Nahuatl term that is even less extensively known than *atole* is the word *esquite* which is used locally among some North Americans of Mexican origin,

for sweetened popcorn. It is not necessary for me
to point out that *popcorn ball* is a well known Americanism for an article of food basically similar to the
esquite of some of our neighbors in the Southwest.

The Nahuatl Indians, just as the New England
and Atlantic coast Indians, had learned to boil corn in
water to which ashes had been added, and thus prepare a food well known to us as *hominy,* a word we
took over from the Indians our forefathers found in
Virginia. The Nahuatl Indians called their hominy
by a name which gave rise to the American Spanish
nixtamal, a word the first element of which means
ashes. This word of Nahuatl origin has not made its
way into general use among us, but it has got as far
as Texas, where in some portions of the state it exists as a localism.

The similar procedures followed in meeting the
food situation in the Valley of Mexico and in the
Virginian and New England areas is of course easily
observed from what has been said. The explanation
of this phenomenon is not apparent. Perhaps similar
needs called forth similar responses, but even so, the
similarity in details of technique is difficult to explain without assuming that there was some form of
contact, or that there had in times long past been
some contact, between the Indians in Mexico and
those in Virginia and New England. This is a prob-

lem far beyond our depth, but later in this paper we shall touch upon it again. Just here we may call attention to the fact that there is certainly no resemblance between the languages used in the old Nahuatl region and those used in the Virginia and New England areas. Two words looking more unlike than the Algonquian *rockahominy,* the most likely candidate for the honor of being the source of our *hominy,* and the Nahuatl term *nixtamal* can hardly be imagined.

In commenting upon *nixtamal* I mentioned that its first element is the Nahuatl word for ashes. At that time I refrained from mentioning that its second element is the Aztec word *amalli,* a food name which has passed into wide currency with us. It denotes an article of food made of corn meal and minced meat highly seasoned with red pepper and rolled into a loaf about the size of a biscuit and baked in wet corn husks. The seasoning used in this food gave rise to another name, *hot tamale,* for it. *Hot tamale* in addition to being used with reference to this food, has also been employed as a mere intensifying ejaculation. The embellished expression *hot tamale, Billy Goat!* has been used, especially by exuberant youngsters, with results quite as satisfying as those obtained from outright profanity.

The brewing and drinking of ardent spirits is not a vice restricted to those who enjoy a relatively high degree of culture. The Mexican Indians were able to obtain from various species of agave a fiery liquor which they called *mexcalli*. From the roots and fleshy leaves of agave they likewise prepared a food which they knew by the same name. The food never made much appeal to American frontiersmen, one of whom said of it that in appearance it resembled, when dried, a mass of soft sole leather, and tasted much like ripe sugar cane. The liquor was never praised, even by those who, in the absence of better, made use of it for their solace and comfort. The word *mescal,* however, derived from *mexcalli,* has become firmly fixed in the language. In addition to its use as a common noun it has been taken up as a place name. There is a Mescal, Arizona, and Mescala, and Mescalero are used as place and river names in the Southwest. Perhaps the use of the word in the name of the principal character in a comic strip, Mescal Ike and Pa Piffle, is also worthy of mention.

In addition to names of food and drinks, words denoting plants passed early from the language of the Aztec Indians into that of their conquerors. It often happens that a word in passing from one language to another is greatly modified in its spelling and pronunciation. Those words that we have obtained from the Aztec Indians have been subjected usually to the process of passing through Spanish on their way to us, so the distortion to which they have been liable has been two-fold in nature.

In Mexico there was a tree which the Indians valued highly, because, for one thing, they obtained from its inner bark the material of which they made paper. The Indians accordingly gave the tree a name which means 'paper tree.' The Spaniards who heard the Aztecs pronounce the name of this tree wrote it in various ways, *anacahuite, anacahuita, anacua,* which in time gave rise to our borrowings, *anacahuite* and *anaqua.* These words are book terms rather than expressions used by the people. Texans in that part of the country where a name for this particular kind of fig tree is needed, operated on this old Aztec word in such a manner as to convert it into *knackaway,* or, as Webster records it, *knockaway.* With the assistance of only a little imagination it is easy to see how a distortion of such proportions as indicated here could have taken place.

The Aztecs made use of a kind of wild gourd to which they gave the quite simple, to them, name *tzilacayutli,* meaning 'smooth gourd.' The flesh of this gourd was prized as food by the Indians, and the Spaniards also found it extremely palatable. The inner portion of this particular kind of gourd or pumpkin is so fibrous that after it is cooked it resembles a mass of hair, and the Spaniards called this delicacy *cabellos de ángel,* 'angel hair.' The Mexican form *chilacayote,* derived from the native name for this gourd, has been taken over into American English, and is applied to several Mexican and Southwestern gourds the pulps of which are edible. According to the *Century Dictionary,* there is a form of this same Nahuatl word, *chilicothe,* used in California as the name of several wild cucumbers that have enormous tuberous roots, on account of which they are sometimes called *man-root,* or *old-man-in-the-ground.*

Two statements of a most surprising nature have been made concerning these two words, and the gourd-like or cucumber-like plants denoted by them. A quite reputable lexicographer says that the Mexican gourd which the natives called *tzilacayutli* or smooth gourd originated in Asia.[20] If this is true, the question at once arises as to how the plant reached this country? Obviously it had to be brought, but by whom? Apparently by the ancestors of the Aztecs.

So far as the California variant, *chilicothe,* is concerned, one student has suggested that it is the same word we have in the Ohio place name, *Chillicothe.*[21] This is a most surprising statement, but unfortunately for the story-value of the matter it would take a great deal of proving to show that the Cali-

fornia term and the name of Chillicothe, Ohio, have
the slightest connection. Our best authorities inform
us that *Chillicothe* was the name of one of the four
tribal divisions of the Shawnee Indians. As these
Indians retreated before the encroachments of white
settlers several villages bearing their name were occupied and abandoned in succession. The meaning
of the tribal and village name is, unfortunately, un-
known.

As a rule, lexicographers keep abreast of each
other by the old and sure method of reading and borrowing from each other's works. This procedure usually works out well for all concerned, especially for
the user of a good modern dictionary, but it sometimes leads to the perpetuation of error. At any
rate, whenever reputable dictionaries disagree funda-
mentally the fact is worth noticing. Such a disagreement occurs in the case of the name of a Mexican plant which played a conspicuous part in the life
of the Indians. One thing which everybody knows
about the vegetation of the Southwest and of Mexico
is that cactus abounds in that region. The word *cactus* is of Greek origin and of course does not come
into this story.

But the Aztec Indians had a word, *peyotl,* which
they applied to various cacti. A quite dependable
dictionary explains the Nahuatl word *peyotl* as mean-

ing literally 'caterpillar,' and as used of these cacti because the downy center of what are known as mescal buttons, the dried tops of a particular kind of catcus, are suggestive of a caterpillar. Another dictionary explains the Nahuatl word as meaning 'that which deceives or gives valor to.'[22] According to this authority, the Indians applied this name to various cacti because they made from these plants a kind of ointment with which they rubbed their legs to make them more impervious to weariness. They also obtained from the plant a powerful narcotic liquor which enabled those drunk upon it to have visions and to see into the future.

No matter what the force of the Aztec word might have been to the natives who used it, the word *peyote* came into American English a century ago and its place in the language is secure. Naturally, its use is generally restricted to the Southwest, and to those who, like botanists, have need of the word. The *Century Dictionary* records the diminutive, *peyotillo,* as the name for a small spineless cactus resembling the peyote.

All those who have read books of western adventure have come upon the term *mesquite.* This is an Aztec name for an important leguminous tree, often no more than a shrub, which grows from California southward to Chile, and produces edible bean-like pods. Since its entry into American English more than a century ago, *mesquite* has been used in numerous combinations, as *mesquite bean, mesquite chaparral, mesquite grass, mesquite root, mesquite thicket, mesquite tree, mesquite wood,* and no doubt others. The word has been variously spelled, as *mezquite, mesquit, mosquit, musquit,* and in frontier usage, through the influence of the well known 'mosquito,' *mesquito, masketo.*

The common jimson weed is perhaps as widely known as any plant in this country. Botanists have not yet agreed on whether it originated in Asia or not. If it did originate in Asia, then we are confronted with the problem of how it managed to get into this country in time to be on hand at Jamestown to greet the first white settlers there, and also how it managed to get into Mexico, presumably before the Spanish conquerors arrived. In Texas the jimson weed has the Mexican name *toloache,* which is just about the same as that which the Aztecs gave it. The Aztec name is made up of two elements which when taken together signify 'to bend the head reverently.' The narcotic properties of the plant account for this native name. Anyone who by accident or design partakes of a concoction made from toloache will no doubt find his head bending over in a very pronounced, if not reverent, way. Some soldiers who came to Virginia in very early times are said to have eaten ignorantly of the plant, whereupon they "were rendered apish and foolish, as if they had been drunk, or were become Idiots."[23]

One of the more recent words with which we in this country have augmented the resources of the English language has an etymological descent of more than usual interest.

In various parts of the old Aztec area there still grows a tall coarse bulrush the leaves of which are used by native Indians for making mats, curtains, and other things. The Aztecs named this weed *tollin,* or *tullin.* The Spaniards took over the name in the form *tule,* and in this form it passed from their language into English in that region. Spanish speakers, proceeding in accordance with the genius of their language, called a place overgrown by the bulrushes a *tular,* the plural of which is *tulares.* In one part of California there were formerly so many of these tulares that when a county was formed embracing a great many of them, the county was named Tulare county, by simply dropping the *-s* of the Spanish plural.

In the wake of the 1906 earthquake in California there occurred in and about San Francisco some cases of bubonic plague. In an effort to combat this disease Doctor George W. McCoy, of the United

States Public Health Service, was sent to San Francisco to have charge of a plague laboratory. Doctor McCoy and his assistants began in 1908 to examine rats and ground squirrels for evidence of bubonic plague. In the course of their investigations they discovered that ground squirrels in Tulare county were dying at a remarkable rate, but not from bubonic plague. The disease they were suffering from was caused by an organism which those working in the plague laboratory succeeded in identifying, and to which they gave the name *Bacterium tularense,* from the name of the county. At that time no name was given the disease which was proving so fatal to the ground squirrels, but Doctor McCoy referred to it as a "plaguelike disease of rodents," in an account which was published in 1912.

There the matter rested for some half dozen years. Early in 1919 what was often called *deer-fly fever* was causing such concern in Millard county, Utah, that the State Health Commissioner appealed to the United States Public Health Service for assistance in investigating it. Doctor Edward Francis was accordingly dispatched to the scene and after careful and brilliant work discovered that what had been known variously as *deer-fly fever, rabbit fever, rabbit disease,* and "a plaguelike disease of rodents" were all caused by the same organism, namely *Bac-*

terium tularense. Accordingly in 1921 Dr. Francis wrote an epoch-making paper on what he had found out, and for the first time used the term "tula-raemia," as he wrote it, for the disease caused by *Bacterium tularense.*[24]

In this way, an old Aztec word, with the assistance of an earthquake, innumerable rats and ground squirrels, and the devoted labors of skilled scientists, passed into use as the foundation of a term that is now well known throughout medical circles, and is more and more percolating into the speech of the laity.[25]

During the past century and a half there have been several Nahuatl words taken up in American English as the names for various animals and birds with which the Aztecs were well acquainted and to which they gave the same names which we use today. Most of the words belonging here, however, are localisms, or are known only to students of nature.

California miners and Texas ranchmen often catch and make pets of a little cat-like animal resembling a raccoon. This creature has a variety of names, his native Aztec one being *cacomistle*. This name, etymologically considered, signifies 'half lion,' the Aztecs in naming this little ring-tailed cat using their word for half, *claco*, and *miztli*, the name they gave to the puma or American lion.[26]

Our best known animal name of Nahuatl ancestry is *coyote*. The evidence indicates that this name for the western barking wolf was known to those English speaking people who were familiar with Spanish sometime before the word was taken up here, but its currency in American usage is undoubtedly the result of a new borrowing from American Spanish and does not represent a continuation of earlier British use. The word is of wide currency in this country and has developed several meanings in addition to that of the well known animal. It was formerly applied to Dakotans as a nickname, but in that use it has not maintained itself. Cowboys sometimes refer to a horse as a coyote if his color suggests that of the little wolf. We sometimes make use of the word to refer to a sneak or contemptible person. Miners formerly used such expressions as *coyote diggings, coyote hole,* in allusion to mining excavations suggestive of diggings made by coyotes, and they made a verb of the word, using *coyote* in the sense of to dig or tunnel somewhat in the manner of a coyote in making its den or hole.

Although the dictionaries have not recognized the word, a name for the mockingbird which turns up frequently in the Southwest is *sin-sontle*. This is the name the bird obtained among the Aztecs, and means 'many-voiced,' in allusion to his capacity as a mocker.

In the valley of the Rio Grande and thence southward there is a large gallinaceous bird, said to be
the only representative of its particular family in the
United States. This bird is some twenty-three inches
long and has a wingspread of more than two feet.
It is easily domesticated. Its name, *chachalaca,* is
the same one that the Aztecs gave it centuries ago,
the word *chachalaca* being, like our *pewee, whip-
poor-will,* and many others, imitative of the bird's
note.

Some years ago efforts were made to get this fine
bird to take up on Sapelo Island, Georgia, and a shipment or two of them, rounded up from natives in
Mexico who had made pets of them, were sent there.
A naturalist who was on hand when these birds arrived found that they were even tamer than chick-
ens, not hesitating to climb about on him, and to
take vigorous pecks at any bright thing like a button—or an eye!—that attracted their curiosity. It
is to be hoped that they have done well in their new
home.[27]

Many of the terms borrowed in this country from
the Indians of Mexico are of a miscellaneous nature, not fitting into any of the categories so far
mentioned. And some of these borrowings are well
known. For example, all those who use chewing
gum, and many who do not, are acquainted with the

word *chicle*. It is a Nahuatl term, and Webster suggests that it may be connected with the Nahuatl word meaning saliva.

Cowboys, especially those of a former generation, used what they called a *McCarty*. This was a hair rope, usually one for tying or leading. Such a rope can not well be used as a riata, as it kinks too easily and is too light to throw. This peculiar name, *McCarty*, is the cowboy version of *mecate*, a word taken over from the Spanish into which language it came from the Nahuatl *mecatl*. Native Mexicans used it as the name of a rope made of vegetable fiber.

Everybody who goes to Mexico or reads anything about the country learns about tortillas. The flat dish or stone upon which these are cooked is called a *comal*, a term only slightly different in appearance from the Aztec *comalli*, from which it is derived. A household utensil well known among Mexicans is called a *metate*, a word derived from the native name, *metlatl*, of this device for grinding various grains into a powder.

On the old Texas frontier a Spaniard was formerly called in derison a *gachupin*. The route by which this nickname came into existence is not entirely clear, but the following tracing of it seems to be justified. One of the things which impressed the Aztecs about the Spaniards who came among them at the beginning of the sixteenth century was that they wore spurs. This pedal augment was something entirely new to the Indians, and they therefore named the conquistadors by a combinative term, *catzopini,* meaning 'the man with spurs on his feet,' or 'the man who pricks with his feet.'

At first this term did not have any derogatory implication. It made its way into the Spanish language at an early date and was used by Cervantes in *Don Quixote.* In the course of time, however, the word took on a derogatory connotation and it was with that signification that it made its way into American English. It has now passed out of use, but may still be found in earlier writings, and sometimes in the work of those who are writing of times gone by.[28]

When the Spaniards came among the Mexican Indians they found that these natives lived in very poor houses, often of mud or sun-dried brick. The natives had a name for an abode of this kind, and this was, as the Spaniards recorded it, *xacalli.* In the sixteenth century the Spanish *x* was used to represent the *sh* sound we are familiar with in such words as *shore, share, sure.* Consequently, the Aztecs must have been calling such a house as we have described a *shacálli.* In the course of time the Spanish word *xacalli* has been so modified in pronuncia-

tion and spelling as to occur now as *jacal,* pronounced
hakal. This Mexican Spanish word passed into
American English certainly as early as 1838. The
Americans apparently had trouble with the spelling
of it for sometimes they spelled it *jacal,* and sometimes *hackal.* How they may have pronounced it a
century ago is a matter for conjecture, though the
spelling *hackal* indicates that they were following
the modern Spanish pronunciation.

The nearest lineal descendant of the old Aztec
xacalli in Spanish is the term *jacal,* but there is no
doubt that in our word *shack,* used of a house, we
employ a term which preserves the original sound of
the native word. As late as 1890 in a Chicago news-
paper the following passage occurred: "I found lots
of families living in the most miserable shackles."
Although it turns up late, it is quite likely that
shackles is a more ancient form than our modern,
widespread *shack.*

2 · Some Muskhogean words in the Southern Vocabulary

In THIS LECTURE we shall devote attention to a few of those words that long ago passed from the speech of the Muskhogean Indians into the language of their conquerors and dispossessors. It is not unfitting that an address of this kind should be given here in what was once the homeland of these Indians, and that it should be given by one who was born and brought up in an area where in days long gone by the Muskogees raised their wigwams and played out their roles on a stage where we all are but as actors for a day.

Some of the words that you and I have known longest and that come most easily from our lips are Muskhogean words. Many of the stories that we listened to most eagerly in those day, pretty far off for some of us, when we were doing our best listening, with most permanent results, were stories of Muskhogean Indians. Because of this background, I am sure that many of us will take no small pleasure in directing our thoughts toward those who have, perhaps without our realizing it, made their contribution to the enrichment of our existence.

The Muskhogean family of Indians received their family name from *Muskogee,* the native name of the principal tribe among those composing this group of Indians. The principal tribes making up the Muskhogean stock were the Alibama, the Apalachi, Chickasaw, Choctaw, Muskogee or Creek, Koasáti, Seminole, Yamacraw, and the Yamasi. The area occupied by these Indians was a fairly extensive one, though it is by no means easy or even possible to indicate its precise boundaries. In general it may be said that the Muskogees occupied the territory extending from the Savannah River and the Atlantic Ocean as far west as the Mississippi River, and from the Gulf of Mexico on the south to the mouth of the Tennessee River on the north.[1]

For those of us particularly interested in Alabama history, it is well enough to bear in mind that, in general, the Creeks occupied the southeastern, the Chickasaws, the northwestern, and the Choctaws the southwestern portions of our state. Coming a bit nearer home for some of those present, the area now embraced in Shelby county seems never to have had a very large population of Indians within its borders. The oldest French and English maps of this region do not indicate that there were any large centers of Indian population here, but in the valley of the Coosa to the east of us there were many Creek Indian vil-

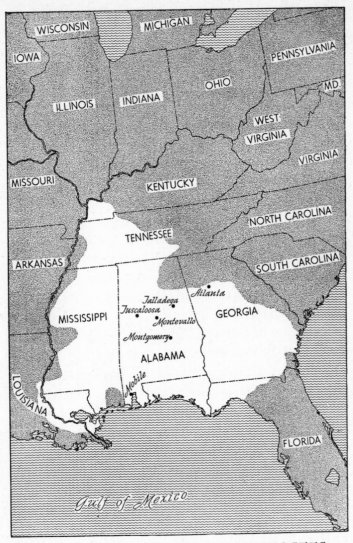

AREA ONCE OCCUPIED BY MUSKOGEES

lages on the Shelby county side of the river. While the Coosa River is usually regarded as having formed the boundary of the Creek lands, not a few indications have been found that there were also Creek settlements west of the river.

One indication that there were Creeks west of the Coosa in early times is that in the treaty of Fort Jackson, in 1814, it was stipulated that those Creeks west of the river should return to the eastern side, so as to be within the proper bounds of the Creek nation. In the main, however, Shelby county lay in the area occupied chiefly by the Choctaws. Indeed, it is thought that the name of the Coosa River is derived from a Choctaw word about which we shall have something to say later.[2]

The fact should be mentioned here that the name *Creek* used for the principal tribe of the old Muskhogean family is perhaps in more common use among students and historians than the tribal name *Muskogee*. Unfortunately, no satisfactory account can be given of the origin or significance of the word *Muskogee*. The idea has been advanced that the word is itself of Algonquian origin, and that the basic meaning of it was something like 'swamp' or 'a region of swamps.' Other scholars have vigorously dissented from this view without, however, being able to offer any explanation of their own.[3]

It is believed that the name *Creek* is one conferred upon these Indians by the white people who observed that there were many creeks in the region occupied by them. It is hardly necessary to point out that this is a somewhat lame explanation of the source of the name. If the first white people who came among these Indians had been impressed by their living in a region abounding in creeks, then obviously the name *Creekers* would have had an appropriateness that is entirely absent in *Creeks.*[4]

So far as the words we have borrowed from these Creek or Muskhogean Indians are concerned, the vast majority of them are proper names. It will be well, therefore, to give here some indication of the significances of the tribal names thus far mentioned, but to which no special attention has been directed.

Apalachi, the name of a Muskhogean tribe, may mean according to the analysis of the word into its parts 'the people on the other side.' The word has been regarded as the basis of the Florida place name Apalachicola, a name which etymologically speaking would thus refer to people living on the other side (of a stream.) However, a radically different explanation of this name will be mentioned later.[5]

Chickasaw, a word with which we Alabamians are perhaps more familiar than we are with *Apalachi,* is unfortunately one the meaning of which can not be made out. The suggestion has been made that it may signify 'rebellion,' and refer to a separation of the Chickasaws from the Creeks and the Choctaws.[6] The same unsatisfactory report has to be made on *Choctaw,* a word with which I am sure all of us have been familiar from our youth up, but the meaning of which is a matter of speculation. Some students have thought it might be a corruption of the Spanish word *chato,* meaning flat, and have in it an allusion to the former practice of the Choctaws of flattening the heads of their babies. Professor Halbert, to whom reference will be made again later on, thought the name might signify 'separation' and refer to an ancient breach between the Choctaws and the Chickasaws.[7]

Seminole, is a Creek Indian word meaning 'separatist.' It was first applied to a Florida Muskhogean tribe which originally consisted chiefly of immigrants from what is now Alabama and southern Georgia.[8] Other tribal names in the list we have given we may well dismiss from further discussion. The tribes known as the Koasáti, Yamacraw, and Yamasi may have at one time been of considerable size, but if so, they long ago ceased to have much importance. By 1891 the Koasáti tribe numbered only four families, or about twenty-five individuals, and lived at the time near the town of Shepherd, San

Jacinto county, Texas. Of the Yamasi, none were known to be surviving at that time.[9]

It will be desirable for us, before taking up for examination any more Indian names, to get clearly in mind some elementary, though not generally known, facts about the languages of those Indians whom the Europeans found here upon their arrival more than four hundred years ago.

During the colonization of the country by Europeans there were encountered north of Mexico no less than 45 distinct and separate language stocks or families of languages in use among the Indians. Some scholars place the number of these distinct and separate languages as high as 55. These languages show no relationship whatever with each other. Accordingly they do not furnish any grounds for our thinking that perhaps all of them came originally from some one parent language. Each of these language groups or families or stocks had a greater or lesser number of dialects. As many as 75 dialects have been made out for one of the language stocks. By adding up all the dialects of all these 45 or 55 languages we find there were no less than 600 of them.[10]

Unfortunately for understanding these Indian languages, there was no written literature in any of them. There was no way of learning an Indian language other than by going among the Indians and studying their speech at first hand. Traders who lived with the Indians picked up a few expressions and some of them were able, after a time, to speak the language of one or more tribes. In some instances traders lived among the Indians, marrying Indian wives and becoming quite expert in the language of those with whom they dealt. Some of these traders wrote down lists of the Indian words they knew. Many of these lists were ultimately published in some form or another, but many more were lost altogether or exist, if at all, in manuscript form.

Among the most industrious students of Indian languages, however, were missionaries. Two missionaries of the many who labored among the Indians of the Muskhogean stock are particularly deserving of our grateful remembrance for the information they left us of the languages of the Creeks and the Choctaws. I take pleasure in here calling attention to these devout men who spent their lives for the moral and physical uplift of their red brothers. Our histories are filled with the names of those who obtained distinction by their success at destroying Indians, but they are often entirely silent about those who devoted a life-time of consecrated and conscientious labor for the uplift of these children of the forest. Indeed, they were of those of whom the world was not worthy, but for whom a crown of righteousness was a just reward.

The missionary to whom we owe the most for our knowledge of the language of the Choctaw Indians was the Rev. Cyrus Byington. He was born of poor parents at Stockbridge, Berkshire county, Massachusetts, March 11, 1793. In 1819 he was licensed to preach, and at that time hoped to go to the Armenians in Turkey to do missionary work. Late in the summer of 1819, however, he was sent by the American Board of Missions to the Choctaw Indians in Mississippi. He labored among these Indians for nearly fifty years, and with his fellow workers succeeded in achieving a remarkable measure of success in his efforts to redeem that nation from drunkenness, ignorance, and immorality.

During his long service among the Choctaws, Byington translated into their language many edifying works, including portions of the Bible, hymns, etc., and wrote a grammar of Choctaw. The first draft of this manuscript was completed in 1834, but he continued to work at it as long as he lived. On his birthday in 1864 after 30 years work on the grammar he wrote in his diary:

The last year I revised the Choctaw Grammar, going over the ground twice. . . . I commit these efforts in my old age to the Lord. I have enjoyed these labours very much. The pleasure of happily resolving difficulties in these studies, and of success in the work is gratifying and reviving to the mind.

Small wonder that a competent critic says of this grammar that it "remains one of the most valuable, original, and instructive of any ever written of an American language."[11]

While he was among the Choctaws, Byington was busily engaged in preparing a dictionary of their language. At the time of his death in 1868 his manuscript containing about 15,000 words passed into the possession of the Bureau of American Ethnology. Alabamians especially should be glad to know that the Bureau in casting about for scholars competent to assist in editing and publishing the Byington dictionary, called upon Henry Sale Halbert, who should be remembered with pride by all his fellow Alabamians. Mr. Halbert was born in Pickens county in 1837, and became one of the foremost authorities on the language and customs of the Choctaws among whom he labored as a teacher for many years. Dr. Thomas M. Owen had such a high regard for Mr. Halbert's character and scholarship that in 1904 he invited him to come to Montgomery. For the last twelve years of his life he lived in the home of Doctor Owen who had secured for him a clerkship in the Department of Archives and History. These two distinguished sons of Alabama, Dr. Owen and Professor Halbert, are buried side by side in Greenwood Cemetery in Montgomery.[12]

The missionary to whom we owe most for our knowledge of the Creek Indian language was the Rev. Robert McGill Loughridge, who was born in South Carolina in 1809, entered the ministry when he was 21, and was selected by the Presbyterian Board of Foreign Missions to minister to the spiritual needs of the Creek Indians. Along with his other writings for the uplift of the Creeks, Mr. Loughridge compiled a Creek-English, English-Creek dictionary. Fortunately this valuable work was published in St. Louis in 1890.[13]

Having paid this deserved but meager tribute to these representatives of that large number of devoted students through whose labors enlightenment about Indian languages has come to us, we may now discuss briefly a feature of the Muskhogean languages which, it is believed, characterized many of the American Indian forms of speech, and one which adds greatly to the difficulty of our understanding the significance, in the minds of the Indians, of certain terms that we have taken over from them.

The Muskhogean languages were in part polysynthetic. Used with reference to languages, polysynthetic designates those which express extended and complex ideas, not by separate and distinct words, but by the use of affixes, suffixes, or stem modifications. Because of the "exuberence" as one writer expresses it, of such elements in the American Indian languages they have been called polysynthetic, a word from the Greek signifying 'much compounded.'

An example or two of how Indians sometimes expressed their ideas may be helpful in understanding this feature of their speech. An Eskimo so we are told, can take the word which he uses for 'see' and by, what are to him, quite easy and intelligible, modifications of it by means of suffixes or affixes or both, come up with a word which to other Eskimos who hear it conveys the information which we should have to express by the phrase: 'he only orders him to go and see.' Again, some of the Indians in British Columbia could take for a base their word meaning 'go' and by using certain elements with it, they could express in one word an idea for which we would have to use the sentence: 'He went with him upward in the dark and came against an obstacle.'[14]

Perhaps these examples will help in making this idea of polysynthetic languages somewhat clearer. In English we express the various notions and relations into which a proposition or complex notion may be analyzed by the use of separate and distinct words. We speak of our language therefore as being 'analytical.' We should not, of course, get the idea that the

Indian languages did not have words in our sense of that term. They did, but along with these they had also an abundance of these cluster words, if we may call them such, which were what we regard as entire propositions or expressions.

When the Indians named anything, as a person, a plant, a tree, a snake, a river, or anything else, they would often make use of one of these cluster words. The process of finding out the significance of an Indian name, therefore, often involves taking apart words that have wrapped up in them these entire complex ideas. It is not difficult to understand that such a dismembering of an Indian name is a task that calls for the best efforts of competent scholars. The whole field of Indian linguistics is pretty badly cluttered up with what are now regarded as entirely impossible explanations of the significance of certain Indian names.

Formerly, for instance, it was thought the name of the state of Kentucky in the Indian language from which it comes, signified 'dark and bloody ground.' The textbooks formerly in use, if they did not expressly convey this misinformation, left an immature reader with the impression that this idea about the significance of the name was correct. Scholars are now agreed that *Kentucky* could not possibly have denoted 'dark and bloody ground,' but that the basic idea in the name is that of 'level,' an idea conveyed by 'kenta,' the Iroquois word which is the basis of the state name.[15]

A similar misconception about the meaning of the name of our own state will be taken up when we come to it. Perhaps the most fanciful of all the attempts to explain the significance of an Indian name is the one recorded about the word *Susquehanna,* a well known river name. This, so we are told, was in former times solemnly derived from the Latin *sus,* meaning pig, *que* meaning and, and *Hanna,* a woman's name, the entire word signifying 'Hanna and her pig.' Later scholars with greater insight into such matters tell us that the proper explanation of *Susquehanna* is 'roily or muddy stream.' Another theory about the significance of the name explains it as meaning a river with long reaches. What the proper interpretation of the name is may never be found out.[16]

We are now better prepared to take up for brief consideration some river names of Muskhogean origin enumerated in a poem some verses of which have lingered in my memory from boyhood. This poem was composed by Alexander Beauford Meek (1814-65), a Southerner who enjoyed at least local celebrity in his lifetime but whose recognition has now become considerably dimmed. He greatly loved the romantic past of the South, and did all he could to instill a similar sentiment in others.[17] This poem on the names of Alabama rivers was included in an oration read by him before the Historical Society of Alabama at its anniversary at Tuscaloosa, July 9, 1855, and later published in his *Romantic Passages in Southwestern History*. Of course there are poems exhibiting greater talent than is displayed in the one under consideration, but it does enumerate very neatly a few of the best known of our stream names of Indian origin.

> Yes! "though they all have passed away—
> That noble race and brave,
> Though their light canoes have vanished
> From off the crested wave;
> Though, 'mid the forests where they roved,
> There rings no hunter's shout,—
> Yet their names are on our waters,
> And we may not wash them out!
>
> Their memory liveth on our hills,
> Their baptism on our shore,—
> Our everlasting rivers speak
> Their dialect of yore!"
> 'Tis heard where CHATTAHOOCHEE pours
> His yellow tide along;
> It sounds on TALLAPOOSA's shores,
> And COOSA swells the song.

Where lordly ALABAMA sweeps,
　　The symphony remains;
And young CAHAWBA proudly keeps,
　　The echo of its strains;
Where TUSCALOOSA's waters glide,
　　From stream and town 'tis heard,
And dark TOMBECKBEE's winding tide
　　Repeats the olden word.

Afar where nature brightly wreathed
　　Fit Edens for the Free,
Along TUSCUMBIA's bank 'tis breathed
　　By stately TENNESSEE;
And south, where, from CONECUH's springs,
　　ESCAMBIA's waters steal,
The ancient melody still rings,—
　　From TENSAW and MOBILE!

We shall take up for brief discussion these names
of streams in the order in which they occur in the
poem.

Chattahoochee is of course the name of a river
which forms part of the boundary between Alabama
and Georgia. The word itself is of Creek Indian origin, and means literally 'marked rocks.' The Indians named the stream because they had found in or
near it rocks that had weathered in such a manner as
to have interesting markings or pictures on them.
Rocks of this kind are found in many places all over

the world. There are at least two places in this country where the presence of such rocks has resulted in place names. There is a place in Michigan called Pictured Rocks, and one in Pennsylvania called Picture Rocks.[18]

Scholars have not been able to tell us much about the significance of the Indian name *Tallapoosa.* Those who have endeavored to dismember the Indian term have not been able to arrive at any better explanation of its significance than 'pulverized rock,' and they have ventured no guess as to what may have caused the Indians to bestow such a name on the stream. Nor have they been able to do much better with regard to the name of the *Coosa* River. The first Europeans ever to enter the beautiful valley of the Coosa were the Spaniards under De Soto. On July 16, 1540, a little more than four centuries ago, De Soto and his followers entered a large Upper Creek Indian town a little less than a mile east of the Coosa River in what is now Talladega county. The name of this Indian town was something very like *Coosa,* and it is thought that this settlement was so prominent that the river took its name from the name of the town. So far as scholars can find out, the word which inspired the town name and led on to the naming of the river was the Choctaw word *kusha,* meaning cane or canebrake.

The stream known as the Alabama River received its name from the Indians, the *Alibamons,* as the French called them as early as 1702. These Alabama Indians were in early times settled along the upper reaches of the river which bears their name,—a stream which begins at the confluence of the Coosa and the Tallapoosa, some dozen miles below Wetumpka, and flows a little over three hundred miles to join the Tombigbee about forty-five miles above Mobile.

The name *Alabama* first used of these Indians has given rise to interesting speculations on the part of scholars. There was formerly current a romantic story to the effect that an Indian chieftain somewhere to the eastward of our state, warred upon and harrassed by the steadily encroaching white settlers, decided to lead his band to a place of rest toward the setting sun. For a long time these Indians threaded their way through the forests and across the plains, hoping to reach a place where they would be forever free from land-hungry white men. Finally, at the close of day, just when the rays of the departing sun were lighting up to best advantage the beautiful and fertile valley of the Coosa, these weary Indians came upon the region which they all felt at once was their long hoped for Eden. Whereupon the leader of the Indian band struck his spear deep into the rich grassy sward and uttered the one sententious word *Alabama!* meaning 'here we rest!'

This story, minus some of the flourishes I may have added to it, was widespread, and succeeded in getting itself alluded to on our former state seal, where, as you remember, the words "Here We Rest" occurred. The result of this situation is that away from here, among people said to be much more energetic and enterprising than Alabamians usually are, our state is sometimes referred to as the 'here we rest' state, with implications that we do our full share of resting here.[19]

It is too bad to give up this pleasant story, but scholars who have gone further into the matter than had those who wrote the textbooks formerly in use, have reached the unamious conclusion that there is absolutely no foundation for the 'here we rest' theory about the name of our state. *Alabama* comes from a Choctaw Indian word, the significance of which is nothing more romantic than 'to trim, cut, gather, plants or weeds.' With the assistance furnished them by the name scholars have arrived at the conclusion that the Alabama Indians were so called because they were thicket clearers or vegetable raisers, or touching the bottom rung on the ladder of prosaicness, 'pea-patchers.'[20]

Cahaba, the name of a rather inconsequential

stream which flows into the Alabama over in Dallas county, is thought to be a Choctaw Indian word meaning 'above water,' but why such a word was ever associated with the stream has not been made out.

There is not at the present time any stream in Alabama called the *Tuscaloosa,* but when the Indians were here one of their names for the river which we now call the Warrior or Black Warrior was *Tuscaloosa.* On an old map of 1733 the river is called "Tuscaloosa R." Much earlier than this, however, De Soto, much to his ultimate sorrow, made the acquaintance of a Choctaw Indian chief named Tascalusa. It may be that the Indians perpetuated the name of this noted chieftain in the name of the river. The significance of *Tuscaloosa* is 'black warrior,' and in arriving at the present designation for the river our ancestors merely translated the Indian name, a procedure that has often been followed in similar circumstances.

As we shall have occasion to mention later on, Indian terms were quite difficult for Europeans to pronounce and it was often easier for white people to translate an Indian name than to try to pronounce it. For example, there is a creek in Russell county called Broken Arrow Creek. This name is apparently the translation of the Creek Indian name for the stream.

The Indians presumably named it as they did because along it they broke reeds for making arrows. Similarly, on the west side of the Tombigbee River, in Sumter county, there is a place called Black Bluff. The Indians are thought to have called it by a name which expressed this idea because in that locality there was a kind of coal which attracted their attention.

Getting back now to the list of Indian names occurring in the poem by A. B. Meek, we take up the word *Tombigbee,* perhaps the most interesting in the entire list. Among some of the Indians in Alabama, particularly the Choctaws, it was customary to expose the dead in the open air until decomposition had so far advanced as to make it possible for old men known as bone-pickers to take the corpses and carefully scrape away the flesh from the bones. The flesh was cast away into some stream or other water, and the bones thus cleaned were preserved in crude boxes or coffins. The river name *Tombigbee* is believed to signify, in the Choctaw language, 'the place where coffins are made.' Apparently the material of which the Indians made these coffins or boxes was easily obtainable at some place or places on the Tombigbee, and the river received its name from this fact.

Some scholars take a slightly different view of

the matter, and regard the river name as having meant among the Indians something like 'coffin makers.' They regard it as likely that those who made boxes for the Indian dead lived along the Tombigbee in Indian times.[21] So far as I know, this is the only river name in our country which alludes to a burial custom on the part of the native red men.

The next name, *Tuscumbia,* is somewhat puzzling. It apparently refers to a stream, possibly the present Tuscumbia Creek in Colbert county, or perhaps to Tuscumbia River over in Mississippi, flowing into the Tennessee. The name Tuscumbia is said to be that of a noted Cherokee warrior, but his name is usually translated 'warrior killer,' and is thought to be of Choctaw or Chickasaw origin. It is somewhat odd that a noted Cherokee warrior should be handed down to posterity by a Choctaw or Chickasaw name. But in the realm of Indian names one gets accustomed to strange things.

The name *Tennessee* has so far baffled the best efforts of our scholars. The belief at present is that it comes from one or more Cherokee settlements named *Tanasi,* but there has not been found in the Cherokee language any root for such a name as *Tanasi.* There is a possibility that *Tennessee* is derived from the Creek Indian word *talasee,* meaning 'old town,' and appearing quite distinctly in the well known name of Tallahassee, Florida. It is known that Tennessee was historically Cherokee and not Creek territory, but there were in its confines Creek settlements that were later occupied by Cherokees.[22]

The next name on our list, *Conecuh,* takes us entirely across the state, this term being the name of a river in southern Alabama that flows into the Escambia River in Florida. The name *Conecuh* has been the subject of quite a bit of speculation on the part of scholars. It is not clear which Indian language, Choctaw or Creek, the word is from. If it comes from the language of the Creek Indians, then the best interpretation of it is 'near canebrakes,' but if it is a Choctaw word the best guess as to its meaning is something like 'there are young canes down there.' One scholar derived the name from the Creek Indian word for crooked, and another regarded it as meaning 'land of canes.' Professor W. S. Wyman, who will be mentioned again later, explained *Conecuh* as coming from two Creek Indian words meaning 'polecat's head.' These attempts to explain the name illustrate the difficulty, already mentioned, of so analyzing Indian terms as to bring forth entirely satisfactory explanations of their original significance.

Escambia, the name of one of our better known rivers and of a county, is a Choctaw Indian word, and means something like 'the stream where there are canes,' or 'the stream in which canes are gathered.'

Tensaw, the name of a river in Baldwin county, perpetuates the name of a small Indian tribe which has long since become extinct. In 1682 the small tribe known by the name of the *Taënsa* were living on the shores of Lake St. Joseph, in the present parish of Tensas, in Louisiana. They apparently often changed their place of habitation. Neither the origin nor the significance of their name can be made out.

Obviously, French influence has played upon the word, for in geographies and gazetteers it is spelled *Tensas,* but the pronunciation quite generally followed is better shown by the spelling *Tensaw.* This word, therefore, reminds us of other place names where the written forms of the words show French spelling, but the pronunciation of which sometimes reveals and sometimes obscures this French influence. For example, in the name of my adopted state, *Illinois,* we preserve the French spelling and pronounce the word with the omission of the final *-s,* just as is usual in French. On the other hand, we spell *Arkansas* with a final *-s,* after the French manner, but in our efforts to omit this *-s* from pronunciation we have evolved a terminal sound such as that heard in *law,* with the result that our usual pronunciation—but by no means the only pronunciation heard for that name—is not represented properly by the spelling of the word. A similar situation prevails with respect to our much less well known word, *Tensas*, pronounced *Tensaw,*—a situation which serves as a pleasant reminder that French settlers had no small share in developing the southern part of Alabama.

Mobile, the last name on our list, reminds us even more strongly of the French settlers here in the days of old Fort Conde de la Mobile. Spanish and French explorers were the first Europeans to come in contact with the Indians whose name is preserved in that of our river and seaport. When Europeans first came among them the Mobile Indians were living just below the junction of the Alabama and Tombigbee rivers. The first efforts to write down the name of the Indians resulted in such words as *Mauvila, Mauilla, Mobile.* The name itself is believed to be connected with a Choctaw word meaning to row or paddle. Consequently the name *Mobile* signifies 'the rowers.'[23]

Anyone who gives even superficial attention to Indian names, as we are doing here, is likely to be impressed by the prosaic nature of the significations that scholars think were inherent in many of them. In times gone by, and perhaps to a less extent even today, the tendency has been to look upon the native red man (he wasn't actually red) as a very noble fellow indeed. There has frequently been ascribed to him a romantic nature which there is very little evidence he possessed. Scholars in former times were quick to see something beautifully sentimental in various Indian place names, and to conjure up explanations which in the cooler light of later and more accurate knowledge are found to have no basis in fact. We have seen what has happened to former interpretations of names like *Alabama, Kentucky,* and *Susquehanna.*

On the whole, we are justified in regarding the Indian as a prosaic fellow. If he had much romantic imagination, that fact is not revealed in many of his place names. One scholar who has shed much light on many place names of Indian origin claims that among those he has examined there are a few that "appeal not only to the intellect but also to the heart." He lists some examples of these appealing place names. The first of these is *Tickfaw,* the designation of a beautiful little river which flows through a piny region of Louisiana. Our scholar in analyzing this river name feels justified in thinking that it means 'rest among the pines.' This is excellent, if true. Certainly it is a great advance over such a name as *Notasulga,* a name which is thought to have been inspired by the Creek Indians finding some old teeth at the site of the Indian town which once stood there, or *Conecuh,* which as we have seen may have reference to the finding of the head of a dead polecat at the place now so named. Still, *Tickfaw* as a name has about it a harshness that is hardly more than made up for by its melodious interpretation, 'rest among the pines.'[24]

Likewise, there are other Louisiana terms like *Chacahoula* and *Catahoula,* the former meaning 'beloved home,' and the latter interpreted 'beloved lake.' The sentiment in these names compensates for the difficulty of pronouncing them, and in the minds of all right thinking people will do much to compensate for the fact that a beautiful name like *Sylacauga* is believed to have signified nothing more romantic than 'buzzard roost.' If the town of Sylacauga has any enemies, and I trust that it has none, they could hardly have wished off on the place a name which, in its interpretation, has less of charm than is possessed by the expression 'the place where the buzzards roost.' Coming as I do from Chicago I can sympathize fully with the sensitive citizens of Sylacauga, because *Chicago* is thought by some to have meant in its Indian form 'the place of the big skunk.' I have drawn some solace since my sojourn in that city from reflecting that this interpretation of the city's name has pertinent revelancy only to certain disappointing characters who have brought anything but credit to our city.

Opelika gets off much better than Sylacauga. When this place was first settled, about 1836, it was called *Opelikan,* and it was not until 1851 that the present name came into use. The place is thought to derive its name from a Creek Indian expression meaning 'big swamp,'—not to be sure the last word in imaginative elegance, but at any rate a considerable remove in the right direction from 'buzzard roost.'

Autauga has been interpreted as meaning 'land of plenty' but there is really no foundation for such an analysis. The name apparently comes from a Creek Indian term *atigi,* meaning 'border'. The name *Autauga* is closely related, linguistically, to *Talladega.* The source of this name is Creek *talwa,* 'town' and *atigi,* 'border,' literally, 'border town,' a name given to the location by the Creeks to indicate that it was a border town, being located on the border between their lands and those of the Cherokees and Chickasaws.[25]

Analyses of Indian personal names do not reveal any greater tendency on the Indians' part toward the expression of beautiful sentiments. One of the greatest warriors among the Choctaws, and one who lived and died a staunch friend of the white man, was Pushmataha. When his name is analyzed it is said to mean, 'a sapling is waiting for him.' This name was bestowed upon the chief when he was young. It is not at all clear what the idea was in the minds of those who bestowed this euphonious title upon the young man, but it requires very little imagination on the part of any of us conversant with the poor promise of certain young men we have known in our time to imagine that Pushmataha might well have acquired his name because in his youth those who knew him best thought he would be hanged when he grew up and that a sapling was waiting to serve as a gallows for him.[26]

There is less obscurity about the name of the celebrated Seminole Indian chief, Osceola, an avowed and lifelong hater of white men by whom he was scurvily betrayed and done to death.

His name is made up of two Creek words, *asi* and *yahola*. *Asi* meant leaves and had particular reference to the leaves of the yaupon, *Ilex cassine,* or *I. vomitoria,* from which the southern Indians prepared their famous black drink used on ceremonial occasions. *Yahola* was a term found in many war titles. It was the name of a powerful deity whose call was repeatedly uttered by those in attendance upon the chiefs as they sipped the black drink. From this circumstance the call itself became known as *yahola.*

Osceola, therefore, may be interpreted as meaning 'black drink singer,' or, a little less romantically, 'black drink hallooer.'

It is interesting to contrast briefly the use that white people have made of the names of these two outstanding southern Indians, Pushmataha, the life-long friend of the whites, and Osceola, the bitter and avowed enemy. According to the *Century Atlas* Pushmataha is found as a place name in Alabama, Mississippi, and Oklahoma. Osceola, the bitter hater and hard fighter, has had places named after him in Arkansas, Florida, Illinois, Indiana, Iowa, Kentucky, Massachusetts, Michigan, Missouri, Nebraska, Nevada, New Mexico, New York, North Carolina, Oklahoma, Pennsylvania, South Carolina, South Dakota, Virginia, Washington, West Virginia, and Wisconsin. In addition there is an Osceola in Ontario, Canada.[27]

In concluding our discussion of some common river, place, and personal names derived from one or other of the Muskhogean dialects, we may well say a word about the melody inherent in Indian terms. People are sometimes inclined to wax poetical about the charming sound of Indian terms, and to regret that more of them were not incorporated into our English speech. The fact is that there are some seventeen hundred Indian words, other than place names, in the language we use or have used in this country, and in view of the difficulty of Indian phonology it is remarkable that as many as seventeen hundred such words found lodgment in our language. Had the melody of Indian terms been all that it might have been, judged by European standards, there is no doubt but that many more than seventeen hundred would have been taken over into the vocabulary of American English.

Whether a word is melodious or not depends upon many things, but chiefly upon the taste of the one who is doing the judging. No doubt to the Indians their words and languages were quite melodious. To be sure, many of the words which are more or less remotely derived from the speech of Indians are melodious to us, but it is not at all likely that any Indian, if he could be allowed to return to this scene and hear us pronounce such Indian words as those just enumerated, would be able to identify them as Indian words at all. In taking them into our language we have so modified them as to render them quite unintelligible, in many instances, and perhaps in all instances, to the Indians among whom they originated. These changes, modifications, and additions which we have imposed upon our Indian terms probably account for most of the melody which the words possess for us.

The melody in words depends too quite largely upon the time and circumstances under which we first learn them. For example, in the county in which I was brought up I became familiar at an early age with such terms as *Bashi, Tallahatta, Ulcanush, Tattillaba, Satilpa,* and these terms impressed me then, as they still do, as being melodious, but it is not likely that they possess the same appeal for others as they do for me.

One of these words, by the way, underwent a strange metamorphosis. *Satilpa,* the name of a creek in the community where I was born, is a Choctaw word, the significance of which has baffled scholars. It seems to mean something like deer or pumpkin or provisions, but definiteness is not possible in explaining it. Anyway, it appears that some careless scribe in trying to write down the word, probably a new one to him, wrote a term which looked very much like *Satilpa* all right, but he incautiously crossed the wrong letter in trying to finish off the *t* and thus produced a new word altogether *Salitpa,* which still survives as the name of a village in the region of Satilpa creek.

It should be pointed out that the melody of any term depends a good deal upon the one who is doing the pronouncing of it. For example, when one of my sons was in the fourth grade in a public school in

Boston his teacher pronounced our word *Mobile* in three syllables, *Mo-bi-le,* with the accent on the last. To those of us fortunate enough to be brought up in this area such a pronunciation could hardly bring out the melody of the word.

We turn now to a consideration of those few Muskhogean terms other than names that have found lodgment in our language, coming first into English here in the South.

The fact that these terms are few in number calls for comment. One of the reasons for this paucity of borrowing of common terms from the Muskhogean is to be found in the fact that pioneers, before they ever came in contact with these Indians, had already provided themselves with such terms as they might have borrowed from them. For example, the Choctaw Indians had a very good term for a black snake, *sinti lusa,* but certainly as early as 1634 white settlers in this country had come in contact with snakes that were black, and had already out of their own linguistic resources provided themselves with an obviously appropriate term for them. Similarly, the Choctaws had a name, *abaksha,* for what we call a chicken snake, but by 1700 this snake had been met with by settlers who noticed that it frequents hen yards and eats eggs. The name they gave it, *chicken snake,* was so obviously appropriate that there was

no need at all for their taking over the Choctaw
abaksha.

The difficulty, for white speakers, of Indian
names must also have been a deterring factor involved in borrowing terms. One of the most common of our southern snakes is the coachwhip. The
Choctaw Indians had a name for this snake, *ipochi
itimapa,* which, even if our forefathers had needed
it, might have been more of a mouthful for them
than they would have relished. The fame of the
southern mockingbird has gone all over the world.
Undoubtedly all the Indians where this bird is a native had a name for it. The Choctaws called it the
hushi balbaha, a name that could hardly expect much
popularity at the hands of our forefathers, even if
they had needed a designation for this bird when
they first came among these Indians. One of the
first American birds to be met with by the settlers
in this country was the whippoorwill. The name
given him was one which echoed his own note. The
Choctaws apparently similarly gave this bird an
echoic name, calling him *chuckkilakbila.*[28]

To the obstacles just enumerated working against
an extensive borrowing of common terms from the
Muskhogean Indians should of course be added the
fact that so far as most of these Indians were concerned they never, for any considerable length of

time, lived on such terms of intimacy with white people as to promote borrowings of words in either direction.

In the main, plant names borrowed from one or another of the Muskhogean dialects are of restricted use or obsolete altogether.[29] One of the earliest of all the American Indian words to pass into the English language was the Muskhogean term *ássi lupútski,* meaning literally 'little leaves,' but applied by these Indians to the species of southern holly used by them in brewing their famous black drink, of which they partook freely on ceremonial occasions. This Muskhogean name for the holly probably existed in various dialects, and from some one of these the word was taken over into English in the form *cassine* or *cassena.* The first Europeans who came among the southern Indians devoted considerable attention to this term and to the concoction prepared from its leaves. White people, thinking there was some medicinal value in the drink brewed from this holly imitated the Indians in preparing it but found that the preparation they brewed needed sweetening. This element they proceeded to obtain from persimmons. The resultant drink was probably not remarkably palatable, for there is no evidence of the survival of this pioneer beverage.

A very well known tree here in the South is the

catalpa. Mark Catesby, a celebrated British naturalist, made long visits to this country, coming first in
1712, and returning here in 1722. On his second
visit he lived for sometime among the Indians on the
Savannah River, and from some region which he described as the "remote part of the country" he secured some seeds of a tree which he said the Indians knew by some such name as *kutuhlpa,* 'winged
head,' a name which they applied to the tree with
reference to its blossoms.

In this troublesome area of Indian etymologies
there have been some who were inclined to think
that *catalpa* goes back to the Choctaw *katapa,* meaning 'divided.' Others think that *catalpa* was the original form which was in time corrupted to *catawba.*
At any rate, there is agreement to the effect that
catalpa is of Muskhogean Indian origin.[30] From
early times the tree has been popular as an orna-
mental shade tree. In 1785 Washington wrote in his
diary: "Planted . . . two catalpas (large) west of
the Garden House."

There is found in Florida a plant that was well
known by and quite useful to the Seminole Indians
there. They called it the *kunti,* a name which the
white people who came after them took over, spelling
it *coontie* or *coonte.* The Indians valued the plant
because of its root, from which they prepared a kind

of bread, using it as a substitute for corn. Scholars
who are fond of taking Indian words apart to see of
what they are made are of the opinion that the Seminole name for this plant resulted from the putting together of two terms, *kána* (in composition) 'ground,'
and *ata,* 'under,' the resulting name signifying that
the part of the plant they valued grew under the
ground.

In southern colloquial speech there is a term *titi*
used of a small evergreen tree that has showy fra-
grant white flowers. I am not sure that we are always careful to restrict *titi* to this particular tree,
but according to botanical works this is the one,
known also as the buckwheat tree, to which this
name should be applied. Etymologists agree that
titi is a word of Indian origin, and one scholar has
ventured the suggestion that the Indians responsible
for our having this word were an extinct tribe that
once occupied most of the peninsula of Florida. It is
not at all clear, however, that these ancient Florida
Indians were of Muskhogean stock, so it may well be
that a Muskhogean origin for *titi* would be very difficult to maintain. Considering the obscurity in
which the remote ancestry of the term is shrouded,
it would be equally difficult to demonstrate that *titi*
is not of Muskhogean origin, and hence properly included in this survey.

Perhaps the most pleasant sounding of the plant names taken over from the Muskhogean Indians is *wahoo*. The *Century Dictionary* points out that this euphonious name is given to several different plants and trees in the South. Perhaps the one to which this ancient Muskhogean term is more properly applied is the burning bush, but the same name is also used for the winged elm, a small tree with corky winged branches found in the southern states. The tree that I was taught to call *wahoo* was neither of the preceding but belonged to an entirely different genus, being a basswood. Country people formerly used wahoo bark for various purposes. Upon one occasion one of my brothers and I split some wahoo rails, much to the amusement of my father who told us when we reported our day's activity that night at the supper table that we would have to split some more rails the following day as the wahoo ones would rot during the early part of the evening. The wahoo passed somewhat into the folklore of the South, the pioneer's expression for a diet indicative of extremely hard times being "fried buckhorns and wahoo bark."

Of those terms other than place names and plant names that passed from the language of the Muskhogean Indians into the speech of southerners I shall here mention only three.

When the first French explorers came into the Louisiana area they found there a fish the like of which they had not known previously. The Indians, that is, the Choctaws, in the region had a name *sakli,* for this fish, and the French took over this Indian name, but just what form the French name had in the beginning it is difficult to say. The fish in question, the crappie, *Pomoxis annularis,* has a silvery appearance and beautiful white flesh. Because of these characteristics, the French name, whatever it was, was converted by folk etymologists into *sacalait,* i. e. *sac à lait,* meaning literally 'milk bag.'

This word, *sac-a-lait,* when it was included in the *Oxford English Dictionary* caused the editor to venture the suggestion that it was perhaps an etymologizing of some Indian word. In the course of time Dr. W. A. Read, upon whom I have leaned heavily throughout these pages, fortunately rounded up the Choctaw word, given above, which he regards as the source of the modern name.

Long after the Indians in this state were asked to leave their homes here and take up abodes in the new lands assigned them in the West, many of the Choctaws remained on their ancestral lands along the Pearl and Pascagoula rivers. These Indians made frequent visits to Mobile, and a century ago their appearance on the streets of that city was not an unusual sight. Often Choctaw women came in the summer selling berries and roots, and again in the winter selling little bundles of pine kindling.

As these Choctaw women with their little bundles of firewood went among their prospective customers they uttered over and over again, as an invitation to buy, the Choctaw word *chumpa,* meaning 'buy.' From this circumstance the Choctaw girls who indulged in this kind of traffic became known as *chumpa girls,* an expression long since out of use. Among the last of its occurrences was in a drippingly sentimental, highly romantic story written by A. B. Meek, who has been mentioned before in this lecture. The title of Mr. Meek's story is in all respects worthy of his exalted esteem for the noble red men whose virtues he never tired of extolling. He called his story "The Fawn of Pascagoula; or, The Chumpa Girl of Mobile."

In conclusion, I shall devote some attention to the good southern word *bayou,* a word which has about as many pronunciations as it has users. The most concise of the pronunciations I have heard is *buy,* a pronunciation once used in my presence by a Baptist preacher who announced that he intended to go to *Bilerbatry,* from which I gathered that his intention was to go to a little place near Mobile named Bayou Labatre.[31] A scholar who has looked into the pronunciation of *bayou* has decided in favor of "buy-u" and I am quite willing, when Congress passes the necessary legislation forcing all of us to use the same pronounciation, to drop my *bay-u* and content myself forever afterwards with *buy-u*.

The origin of this word was for a long time uncertain. Scholars were inclined to derive it from the French word *boyau,* meaning an intestine or gut. It took considerable stretching of the imagination for them to explain how this somewhat unpleasant meaning of the French word suggested such a body of water as *bayou* denotes. William Darby, an American geographer at the beginning of the nineteenth century, recorded his belief that *bayou* is derived from the Spanish word *bahia* or *baya* meaning 'bay,' but this derivation had so little to commend it that it has not been heard of for a long time.

A little more than fifty years ago Prof. W. S. Wyman, an excellent scholar well versed in the languages used by the Indians who formerly occupied Alabama, solved very neatly and conclusively the problem of the origin of *bayou*. From his researches into the early history of the French occupancy of this southern country, particularly Louisiana, Professor Wyman found that one of the first Indian tribes in the Louisiana area that the French encountered were the Bayogoula Indians, a small tribe of Muskhogean stock, who by war and pestilence had disappeared entirely by 1721. Their name in their own language *Báyuk-ókla,* 'bayou people,' shows similarity with other Choctaw names, as Pascagoula, (from Choctaw *Pask-okla,* bread people); Pensacola, (*Pansh-okla,* the hairy people); Apalachicola, (*Apelach-okla,* the helping people, allies.) For a different interpretation of this last name see p. 136.

Professor Wyman was not only able to identify our word *bayou* in the name of these Bayogoula Indians, but he also found more direct evidence that the word is from the language of the Choctaw Indians. In accounts written by Frenchmen who were in the Louisiana area at an early time he found the term, written in French *bayouc* and *bayouque,* occurring over and over again. The earliest of these accounts was one written by a ship-carpenter who accompanied D'Iberville to Louisiana in 1699. In his account there occurs a passage which translated reads as follows: "Five leagues further and keeping always to the left on the lake [i.e. Pontchartrain] one finds a stagnant stream which the Indians call bayou."

Professor Wyman's article pointed out clearly that the Choctaw *bayuk,* meaning 'a small sluggish stream,' is the source of our term which is now common all over the country. This article also called attention to the occurrence in such names as *Pasca-*

goula, Pensacola, Apalachicola, of the same Choctaw Indian element *okla* meaning people that occurs
in the state name of Oklahoma which is the Choctaw
way of saying 'red people.' Professor Wyman also
pointed out that the Choctaw word *bayuk,* having
passed through the alembic of French pronunciation
and writing accounts for such names among us as
Boguechito, Boguefalala, Boguelisa. In these there
is clearly seen the old Choctaw word *bayuk,* meaning
'a small stream.'

There have been few articles which in short com-
pass shed so much enlightenment as did this one of
Professor Wyman's which appeared in *The Nation*
for Nov. 15, 1894, p. 361. Unlike many an article,
this one convinced all those who read it that the origin of *bayou* need not be sought any further. It takes
a long time however, for error to die out.

In 1945 when H. L. Mencken brought out his *Sup-
plement I* to the fourth edition of his immensely valuable work on American English, I was honored by
being asked to write a review of it for the *New York
Times Book Review.* Being a mere human being
and therefore not able to get every last thing in his
book entirely right, Mr. Mencken failed to point
out, as he should have done, that the origin of *bayou*
had finally been settled once and for all. In my review I was able to point out the origin of the word,

thus contributing a bit of information for which Mr. Mencken wrote me a letter of thanks. My review, however, fell under the highly critical eye of a New York doctor—whether a Ph.D. doctor or an M.D. doctor, or an ordinary horse doctor I do not now recall. At any rate, he was a man of sufficient leisure to take his pen in hand upon reading my review and write me a most scathing letter, calling attention to the affliction brought upon humanity by such smart alecks as myself who know so much that is not so that intelligent doctors like himself are kept busy setting them right. He informed me that the idea that *bayou* is from the Choctaw Indian language was absurdly ridiculous, that it is derived from the French word for gut, and that intelligent people like himself had been in possession of this information for a long time.

For some reason not at all clear to me now, I merely filed this important philological contribution in my waste basket and never informed the New York doctor whose name I have long since forgotten, that if he would take the trouble to look in his Webster's dictionary he could see that I am by no means alone in thinking *bayou* is properly ascribed to a Choctaw Indian origin.

3 · *Africanisms in the Plantation Vocabulary*

$\mathcal{B}$EFORE taking up those terms that came first into the English language here in the South as borrowings from the speech of Negroes, it is desirable that we devote some time to the background of this source of contributions to our language.

African slavery and white slavery entered this country the same year. Perhaps not many of us went through elementary school without learning that in 1619 the first slaves were brought to Virginia, but the fact is not so generally known that in this same year a ship with 100 pauper children likewise unloaded its cargo in the Virginia colony. Since we are not here concerned with the institution of slavery, either white or black, we shall say no more about white servitude in this country, chiefly in New England, but merely mention in passing that our very common words *kidnap, kidnapper,* and *kidnapping,* came into the language with reference to the stealing of white children from various ports in Europe for the purpose of deporting them and selling them for a period of years as slaves in this country.[1]

The importation of African slaves proceeded slowly at first. It is thought that by 1650 there were only 300 Negroes in Virginia. By 1671 there were 2000. By the time of the Revolution there were, according to the best estimates that can be made, about half a million Negro slaves in the American colonies. Before and for a long time after the Revolution the great majority of the Negro slaves were brought directly from Africa, though of course there were a good many brought in from other places, notably the West Indies. In the Convention which framed our federal constitution of 1787 efforts were made to abolish the slave trade altogether. These efforts resulted in a compromise according to which a provision was introduced into the Constitution which virtually provided for the cessation of the bringing in of slaves after 1808. In that year, accordingly, Congress prohibited the further importation of slaves, but a contraband traffic continued until the time of the Civil War.

It is not difficult to gain some idea of those parts of Africa whence the slaves were brought. The nearest parts of the Dark Continent where slaves could be obtained were naturally those frequented by the slave ships. Accordingly, that part of the coast of West Africa extending from the Senegal region to the southern limits of Portuguese West Africa was the one most drawn upon for slaves, not only by those traders coming to this country but also by traders going to all parts of the civilized world of that day. Slave dealers in such places as New York, Charleston, and Savannah, in advertising their human wares, made it quite clear as to where particular shipments came from, or at least were represented as coming from. Such expressions as the following occurring in the advertisements of slaves for sale in the newspapers of that time tell their own story as to the origin of the slaves: "Very prime Congo slaves," "Prime Mandingo Africans," "choice Gold Coast negroes," "prime Windward Coast Africans."[2]

The reasons dealers were particular to indicate the source of the slaves they offered for sale was that Negroes from different parts of the west coast of Africa had different characteristics. Some were quite docile and easily trained, others were more obstinate and slower witted. Some were exceptionally strong and healthy. Those coming from the Congo were regarded as being among the least desirable of all. In the meantime of course, those slaves that had been brought in early, and had grown accustomed to the new environments, had developed prideful attitudes based upon the wealth or social prominence or both of their owners. And as time passed on those Negroes born here had, in addition, a pride of ancestry that caused them to look with contempt or at least with an air of superiority at those newly-arriving from beyond the sea. Those of us who have read Uncle Remus may remember that in the story about Death and the Negro man, Uncle Remus describes the chief Negro actor in that story as being a very incorrigible old man, a real "Affika nigger, bowlegged and bad tempered."

When groups and individuals of vastly different cultural attainments come into daily contact with each other they immediately begin to modify each other's culture. This process of mutual influence began as soon as the first Africans arrived in this country. The ancestral habits and customs, and particularly the language, of the Africans underwent a most radical and abrupt change as soon as they passed under servitude to white masters. At the same time, a very slight influence was exerted upon the white masters from their association with their slaves. In order to appreciate how slight this reverse influence was upon the white people it is necessary to remember the large number of slaves that lived and died here in the South before the Civil War. Generations of them, in numbers that must have run up into the hundreds of thousands, lived in more or less close contact with those who worked and cared for them, and who in some cases to be sure grossly mistreated them, but the traces of Negro influence upon the culture of the white owners is so difficult to detect that perhaps few of us have ever had any reason to suspect that such evidence can be found at all.

Indeed, were it not for some words that linger on in our speech, it would be difficult in the extreme to maintain that there was any influence of any kind flowing from the slaves towards their masters. So far as the resulting language is concerned, however, there are unmistakable traces of influence on the vocabulary, and these we shall presently take up for more detailed consideration. Before doing so we should call attention to two things which greatly worked against the exercise of much linguistic influence from the side of the slaves.

In the first place, it was as a rule impossible for the Negroes to maintain the native languages they brought to this country. They were landed at such places as New Orleans, Savannah, and Charleston, and from such centers they were sold in all directions. The chances for those coming from the same dialect area in Africa getting together in one area in sufficient numbers to make it possible or desirable for them to make any use of their ancestral speech were very slight indeed. The only course for them was to learn as quickly as possible the language of those whom they served.

We are not to suppose of course that regular language instruction was given to the slaves by their owners. In many cases, especially in the very early days, they were brought, in shackles, from the jungle life they had known in Africa, and put to such work as it seemed they could best perform. Their advance in speaking English was a secondary matter about which little care was taken.

Another thing which acted as an impediment in the exercise of African influence on the language of white people was the natural aversion on the part of the dominant class to allow anything in the speech of the slave to become a part of their own vocabulary. Individuals differed greatly of course in the aversion they felt at knowingly permitting terms from the slave lingo about them getting into their speech. This resistance must have been less, however, in the case of the very young, and since it was often the case that the very young were the ones most exposed to the influence of slave speech, we are justified in suspecting that some of the words to be taken up presently may have passed first from the language of the slaves into the vocabulary of white people at a time when the recipients of the new words were quite young.

I am able from my own observation to furnish a good example of what there must have been much of, first and last, throughout the slave-holding states.

When I was a small boy I once heard my father use the word *cooter,* under circumstances which made the meaning of the word quite clear. Accordingly I did not at the time make any inquiry about the term, as a child is likely to do in the case of a new word's coming within the range of his observation. Years later, however, I became very much interested in this word *cooter.* My father had in the meantime passed away, but a sister of his, at that time more than eighty years old, was still available for questioning.

I can remember yet how proud my aged aunt was to inform me that neither she nor her sisters or any other member of her father's household would use *cooter,* and they regretted that their brother Jim, my father, had taken up such a word. She told me that *cooter* was a Negro word meaning a turtle or terrapin, and that Jim had heard "old Nellie," a slave in my grandfather's household, use the term, and had thought little enough of the purity of his speech to use it himself. This aversion to recognized slave influence, operating with the wholesale distribution of the slaves already mentioned, no doubt accounts for the relative meagerness of the impression made upon the southern vocabulary by the speech of Negro slaves.

Fortunately for our means of studying the effects, such as they were, of this influence on vocabulary, an unusual situation prevailed along the coastal area of South Carolina and Georgia. To the so-called rice and indigo islands in this area there were early brought a great many slaves, many of them directly from Africa. They were purchased in large numbers to work on the rice and indigo plantations along the coast and on the islands lying well off the mainland, and extending roughly, from Georgetown, South Carolina, to Florida. It was commonly thought at the time that the climate in these regions was certain death for white people, hence the slaves had very little contact save with their fellows. Many of them lived and died on the islands without ever visiting the mainland, and without ever seeing more than a few white men. Even the overseers were often Negroes.

After the Civil War the descendants of these slaves continued to live on the islands, as they of course do to this day. They constitute one of the most remarkable linguistic groups in this country. They and their speech have aroused interest for the past fifty years or more, and books and articles have been written about them. These Negroes are known as Gullahs or Gullah Negroes, and their dialect is likewise known as Gullah.[3]

About fifteen years ago a careful study of the Gullah Negroes and their speech was undertaken by a

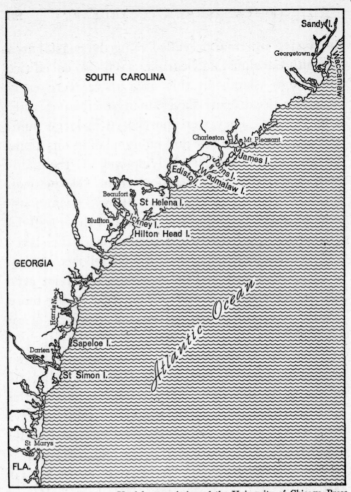

THE GULLAH REGION

WEST AFRICAN SLAVE TRADE REGIONS

brilliant scholar, Dr. Lorenzo Dow Turner, of Fisk University, now of Roosevelt College in Chicago. Dr. Turner went among the Gullahs, and, being himself colored, succeeded in gaining their confidence and sympathetic assistance in his work of studying their speech and customs. He listed thousands of their words, and made phonographic records of many of their songs and stories. Provided with this wealth of material, Dr. Turner then went to such places as the University of London, Paris, and Brazil where he could get in touch with informants coming up to those places from those same areas in West Africa from which the ancestors of the present Gullah Negroes originally came. Dr. Turner enlisted the help of these informants in examining with him his Gullah material and relating it to what they knew of modern African usage. With their assistance and with the help obtained from scores of dictionaries of various African languages, Dr. Turner has made a most revealing study of the speech of the Gullah Negroes. He has written an extremely interesting book embodying what he has learned about Gullah speech, and the corresponding terms in the present West African dialects. In his book Dr. Turner lists more than 4,000 African words still used by Gullah Negroes. In the preparation of this paper I have been extremely fortunate in being able to draw on Dr.

Turner's findings, though as I write his book is yet unpublished. With his accustomed generosity he has provided me with a copy of his manuscript and invited me to make such use of it as I care to, both in this paper and in the dictionary of Americanisms upon which I am now engaged. I shall often have occasion in the following pages to refer to this excellent study.

The fact is well known that the Africans introduced into this country in former times brought with them a large element of superstition. Some of their words which found temporary or permanent lodgment in our speech reflect this phase of the slave's life. Among the Negroes there were certain 'conjure' men known as *obia-men* who carried about with them a staff marked with frogs, snakes, etc. Some of the Negroes imagined that a blow from this magical wand would occasion a long and troublesome disorder, and even death itself.

The African word *obeah* was taken over by white people and used sometimes in writing about superstitions of the slaves. William F. Samford, formerly a man of some importance in the political life of Alabama, writing from his farm near Auburn, in 1866 used the following expression: "Here, in a mile of me, is a negro woman dying, who says an old African hag put a snake in her four years ago, and the Obi doctor has gone to deliver her."[4]

A book on Americanisms that came out in 1871 listed the word *zombi,* and defined it as follows: "*Zombi,* a phantom or ghost not infrequently heard in the Southern States in nurseries and among the servants . . . is a Creole corruption of the Spanish *sompra.*"[5] The information given here about the presence of this word in the southern vocabulary was correct, for Cable in one of his stories spoke of a character who heard "the voice of zombis."

The word is no doubt African, for in the Congo region *zambi* is used to mean a god, and similarly *zumbi* is used to mean a good luck fetish.[6]

Despite our best efforts we Southerners occasionally get *hoodooed.* Sometimes when everything we undertake goes wrong we are sure that there is at least one *hoodoo,* and maybe more, working against us. Scholars tell us that *hoodoo,* both the noun and the verb, is a variant of *voodoo.* According to the best evidence so far found, *voodoo,* the noun and the verb, passed into English use in the New Orleans area, and the prevalence of the word there is undoubtedly to be ascribed to its currency among Africans brought there in early days. In some parts of Africa *vodu* means a spirit, good or bad, and is sometimes used of a tutelary deity or demon. Among the Gullahs *wudu* is used to mean witchcraft, sorcery, a sorcerer. They also use *hudu* in just the way we do.

Formerly in New Orleans there was popular among the Negroes an immodest voodoo dance called the *calinda* in which the men formed one line and the women another facing them. About a hundred years ago the city authorities banished this dance, along with others associated with voodoo practices, from Congo Square in New Orleans.[7]

The word *calinda* has been grappled with by different etymologists, but the results are not entirely conclusive. Webster gives American Spanish as the immediate source of the word, and suggests that the dance was originally an African war dance. No matter what may be the ultimate origin of the word, there is hardly a doubt but that it reached our shores on the lips of African slaves who may, or may not, have brought it from their homeland in Africa.

The Negroes' love of music and musical ability are so well known that it is not surprising to find that some of their words which attracted the attention of their masters had to do with musical instruments. Two such words are no longer used, but it is interesting to examine them.

Just when the war clouds of the approaching American Revolution were hanging low and threatening on the horizon, there came to this country from the Shetland Islands an indentured servant by the name of Harrower who, because of dire poverty, was forced to come to Virginia as a school-teacher, and to stipulate that he would serve in that most humble (at that time) capacity for four years in return for bed, board, washing, and five pounds in money for the four year period.

Harrower kept a diary of his experiences as an indentured school teacher. In this diary he gave the following account of how he spent part of Saturday, December 25, 1775:

At noon went to Newport to see Mr. Martin Heely, schoolmaster to Mr. Spotswood's Children, and after dinner I spent the afternoon with him in conversation and hearing him play the Fiddle. He also made a Neger come and play on an Instrument called a Barrafou. The body of it is an oblong box with the mouth up and stands on four sticks put in bottom, and cross the top is laid 11 lose sticks upon which he beats.[8]

It is clear from this description that the instrument was a kind of xylophone. The base of this queer looking word *barrafou* is the Bambara word meaning xylophone. The word *barra* or *bala* is still used among the Gullah Negroes for a xylophone, and in the Bambara language in Africa the word *fo* means 'to play.' Hence the term *barrafou* literally means 'to play a xylophone.' The observer of this unique musical performance did not observe as carefully as he might the linguistic side of the phenomenon he witnessed, but he more than made up for this deficiency by reporting quite accurately on the nature of the instrument which, he thought, was called a *barrafou*. The real name for it was undoubtedly more nearly *bara* or *bala,* and the odd name *barrafou* resulted from ignorance or carelessness.

The term is of course long since obsolete in our speech, but as I have said, its basic element lives on in the language of the Gullah Negroes.

Just after the Revolution an Englishman was travelling through this country, and finding here an abundance of material for his pen. In one of his chapters he pictured the typical life of a plantation owner, and having disposed of the master he proceeded to describe the life of the typical slave. He mentioned the fondness the Negroes had for music, and told of how a slave, even after a hard day's work, would go off to a dance and take part in the festivities there, "keeping time and cadence, most exactly, with the music of a banjor (a large hollow instrument with three strings), and a quaqua (somewhat resembling a drum)."⁹

The *quaqua* must have been an African instrument. So far as I know, no African word has as yet been found to serve as the antecedent of it, but *kwakwa,* meaning the sound of scratching, is a possible candidate for the honor of being related to this word known to us only through this passage in the works of a British traveler.

Banjo has for a long time been regarded as a word that was contributed to our language, first here in the South, by African slaves. The customary explanation of the origin of the term is that Negroes in the West Indies became acquainted there with a musical instrument which the English called a bandore. The Negroes were very much taken with this instrument, but in pronouncing the name of it they did a slightly imperfect job, with the result that from their mispronunciation the term *banjo* was in time developed. Some of these slaves later coming to the South, brought this word as well as the instrument, of which they were so fond. The word in its mispronounced form passed into currency, probably first being used by the sons and daughters of plantation owners who often had Negroes with banjos furnish music while they danced.

This is a good story, but now that Dr. Turner has completed his study of Gullah it may have to be considerably revised. In the first place, there are puzzling features involved in this story of the transition of *bandore* to *banjo*. For instance, it is surprising that none of the early writers who commented on the Negro and his banjo ever recognized either the word as being a slight modification of *bandore*, or the instrument as being much the same as a bandore. The first example we have of *banjo* occurs in a his-

tory of Jamaica dated 1740. The author speaking of
the Negroes says:

They have other Musical Instruments, as a *Bangil*, not much
unlike our Lute in any thing but the Musick; the *Rookaw,*
which is Two Sticks jagged; and a *Jenkgoving*, which is a
way of clapping their Hands on the Mouth of Two Jars:
These are all played together, accompanied with Voices,
which make a very terrible kind of Harmony.[10]

In a somewhat later work on the West Indies mention is made of "the wild banshaw's melancholy
sound."[11]   These terms, *bangil* and *banshaw,* apparently refer to a banjo, as it is now called, but it is
not easy to regard them as the results of the Negroes' attempts to pronounce *bandore*. A remarkable
man, Jonathan Boucher, well known in his day, while
sojourning in Maryland and Virginia about 1770 became acquainted with the banjo and in one of his
writings described it as "a rude musical instrument,
made of the shell of a large gourd, or pompion, and
strung somewhat in the manner of a violin: it is used
much by negroes."[12]

Thomas Jefferson in his well known work on Virginia, wrote as follows: "The instrument proper to
them [*sc.* Negroes] is the Banjor, which they brought
hither from Africa." In the *Oxford English Dictionary* there is a quotation, dated 1801, written by
Marie Edgeworth: "What is this, mama?—It is not
a guitar, is it?" "No, my dear, it is called a banjore;

it is an African instrument, of which the negroes are particularly fond."

These are only a few of the early references to the musical instrument known today as a banjo. The tenor of all these accounts is the same; they all represent the instrument as typically Negro, and, by implication at least, the word as coming from the language of the Negroes. There has so far not been brought to light any early account which recognizes the identity of the word with *bandore,* or the instrument as being like a bandore. It is as if a number of observers were to go to Africa and find there a musical instrument crudely resembling a piano, and hearing the natives call it a *pi-hanner,* should fail to recognize that it was a kind of piano, and that *pi-hanner* was the same word as *piano.*

If the obstacles just discussed can be overcome by those who insist upon deriving *banjo* from *bandore,* the following excerpt from a letter which Dr. Turner was good enough to write me recently will still have to be taken into account:

The most probable source of *banjo* is the Kimbudu (Angola) word mbanza, an instrument similar to our *banjo.* This word (spelled in Brazil banza) is also used in Brazil for an instrument resembling the guitar, and is generally assumed to be an African word. The word *banjo* (pronounced *banju*) is also used in Brazil, the *j* having the sound of *s* in *measure.*

One would naturally expect that the slaves brought

to this country from Africa would have in their native languages words for creatures they had known
in their homeland, and that at least some of these
would be applied to creatures they found in this new
environment. The evidence shows that this procedure did take place.

As long ago as 1736 an Englishman who made a
voyage to Georgia wrote as follows: "There are
Numbers of the Heron Kind of different Species and
Colours some small ones of the most beautiful White
which are called Poor Jobs, from their being generally very lean."[13] In the latest Webster *poor joe* is
recorded as a name used locally for the great blue
heron.

The evidence is now pretty clear that the *poor Job*
of 1736 and the *poor joe* of the latest Webster are
one and the same expression. Furthermore, the locality in which the great blue heron is called *poor joe*
is those parts of the South where this bird is found.
Furthermore, there is little doubt but that this localism is of African origin. The Gullahs to this day
call the heron *pojo,* and in Sierra Leone and Liberia
whence their ancestors came, this same word occurs
as a name for the heron.

More than a century ago Mrs. Anne Royall was
anathema to many quite respectable people who regarded her as a noisy old crackpot given to black-

guarding in her books and other writings anyone who incurred her ill-will, and her ill-will was easily incurred. This old termagant made a tour through some of the southern states and wrote a book about her travels. In this account, speaking of what she had seen near Augusta, Ga., she wrote: "There are a few larger heaps of earth . . . in the shape (or nearly) of a grave, said to be made by a kind of tarapin, Quagers, or some such name."[14]

Mrs. Royall was in the area of the hardshelled land tortoise or gopher, and her reference must be to that creature. The name *quager* that she found employed for the gopher has not survived. Her use of the term is the only instance of its occurrence so far brought to light. There is not much doubt that her word *quager* is an Africanism. In the Twi language used on the African Gold Coast there is a word *kwakwa*, meaning the sound of scratching. Some form of this word may well be the basis of *quager*. Certainly the southern hardshelled gopher is a mighty scratcher, the common folk-belief when I was a boy being that in scratching or digging out his tunnel-like burrows or dens he doesn't stop until he reaches water.

The term *cooter* has been referred to already as being in my father's vocabulary as the result of a borrowing he had made from the speech of a slave woman in the household of which he was a member.

It is a word for turtle or terrapin which has gained wide currency in the South, and has led to the occurrence in colloquial speech of the verb *cooter,* meaning to loiter, idle, or trifle around.

The evidence is very strong, if not absolutely conclusive that *cooter* is a contribution to our speech deriving from the slaves of former days. At any rate, the word is found not only among the Gullahs, but it is widely current in those parts of Africa that furnished the ancestors of the present Gullah speakers.

The only thing that seems to weigh against the African origin of the word is that it is apparently derived from the verb *to coot,* a verb which goes back in English usage to at least 1667. The source of this verb has never been made out. The noun is represented in the *Oxford English Dictionary* as being derived from this earlier verb. But even if this is the case, it may well be that so far as usage in the South is concerned it was the slaves who derived the noun from the antecedent verb. The prevalence of the noun in Africa however strongly suggests that it was from that region that the noun was brought in the first place, and that without any reference to the use of the verb *to coot.*

The word *chigger* has perhaps occasioned philologists quite as much irritation as the insects it designates have inflicted upon those unfortunate enough to come in contact with them. The *Oxford English Dictionary* s. v. *Chigoe,* records our word as a West Indian name, and records its French and Spanish forms, but is unable to reach any definite conclusion as to its origin. The latest Wester derives *chigoe* from French, and points out that it came into French from the language of some South American Indians. And Webster cites some words, *chico, sika,* the meanings of which are not given, as current among some of the Carib Indians.

The problem of the origin of *chigger* is admittedly a difficult one, but there is a possibility if not a likelihood that its source is African. Dr. Turner found the term in use among the Gullah Negroes in the sense of an insect, a flea. The fact that the Gullahs use the word is of course not by any means proof that the word is of African ancestry. There are many English words in Gullah, and there is nothing to show conclusively that *chigger* may not be such a word.

The fact which is more significant is that this same word *chigger*—in forms not difficult to recognize—is wide-spread among African tribes occupying the areas from which the ancestors of the Gullahs are known to have come, and in its African use the word is applied to the same insect, apparently, which was encountered first by Europeans in the

West Indies area. At any rate, dictionaries such as the Century and the latest Webster appear to be in error in identifying the chigger, the insect, with the West Indies and South America alone. Even if it can be shown that this pest originated in that part of the world, it has not remained there but is now found in Africa. The question of when the insect reached Africa, and whether or not he carried with him his South American name cannot, probably, ever be answered. But it is entirely possible that the creature was in Africa early enough to witness, if he cared to, the departure of the first slaves for the New World, and that at that time he had the name which he still goes by in Senegal and Gambia, in northern and southern Nigeria, in Liberia, and Sierra Leone, and perhaps in other regions in Africa.

The fact should be pointed out that no matter how the word *chigger* got into British English, it would require a good deal of proving to show that it became current in American use as a result of its previous use in British English. It is entirely likely that its American use is to be ascribed to a borrowing from African or South American sources, made in this country.

It is interesting in this connection to notice that certainly by 1763 chiggers were well known in the West Indies, and that by that date the Negro slaves there were practicing a technique in dealing with them that, at least in part, remains in vogue. Grainger writing in 1763 with especial reference to the situation on St. Christopher's, says:

These, by the English, are called chigoes or chigres. They chiefly perforate the toes, and sometimes the fingers; occasioning an itching, which some people think not unpleasing, and are at pains to get, by going to the copper-holes, or mill-round, where chigres most abound. They lay their nits in a bag, about the size of a small pea, and are partly contained therein themselves. This the Negroes extract without bursting by means of a needle, and filling up the place with a little snuff; it soon heals, if the person has a good constitution. One species of them is supposed to be poisonous; but, I believe, unjustly. When they bury themselves near a tendon, especially if the person is in a bad habit of body, they occasion troublesome sores. The South Americans call them *mignas*.[15]

As it was with the names of creatures, so likewise with the names of plants. The slaves must have brought to these shores many names for the plants they were acquainted with in Africa. A few of these terms passed from the speech of the Negroes into the language of their overlords, and some of them have maintained their place to this day.

The word *peanut* originated in this country, but there is nothing African about the origin of this expression. It was arrived at simply by combining two very common words. This name, however, is by no means the only one which the peanut has. In colloquial speech we call peanuts *pinders, goobers,* and *ground peas.* Both *pinder* and *goober* are words of African ancestry. Negro slaves brought both of them to this country. It is interesting to observe that the African word *goober,* meaning peanut, also means, in the Kongo region, kidney, the word being applied to the peanut because of its shape.

Attention should also be called to the spelling *pinda* which is found in Webster's dictionary, the latest edition. This spelling is quite correct, etymologically, for the word comes from the Kongo expression *mpinda,* but so far as I have observed, those who actually use the word do not spell it in this manner. The forms *pinder, pindar,* are the ones actually in use, and the first of these, *pinder,* has found place in the dictionary, being recorded in Webster as a variant of *pinda.*

Another term which arouses interest in this connection is our word *yam,* meaning a particular kind of sweet potato. I call it, in this sense, *our* word because it arose in Virginia at least as early as 1676, and here in the South is the only place where the word is used in the sense we give it. The makers of Webster's dictionary accuse us of calling a sweet potato a yam. They might better explain to their readers that we in the South apply the term *yam* to a particular kind of succulent red-meated sweet potato. People of discriminating and educated taste in such matters usually prefer this particular type of sweet potato, though they have no objection to the white meated dry variety if genuine yams are unobtainable.

Webster also explains that the word *yam* is a borrowing into the English language from Portuguese, the Portuguese having taken their word from African in the Senegal area in West Africa. This etymology may be quite accurate for other portions of the world, but it would be very difficult to show that we, here in the South, derived our word *yam* from the Portuguese, or from anybody who had previously secured it from that source. Our word came to us directly from headquarters, that is from Africa. There was no sense in our bothering the Portuguese for it when we had in our midst the very people who gave the word to the Portuguese. The Gullahs still use *jambi* for a reddish sweet potato, showing that they have retained the word brought here by their ancestors.

It is a weakness on the part of lexicographers to think that when they have explained how a word got into the English language they had accounted for its presence among us in this country. The erroneous assumption which they often go upon is that once the word has been traced into British English, then it naturally follows that we in this country took it from that source. This attitude of mind was well set forth by John Ruskin, a delightful old gentleman who was pathetically ignorant about some things that he wrote of beautifully. For instance, in 1873 he penned the following excellently worded nonsense:

For this dead Venice once taught us to be merchants, sailors, and gentlemen; and this dying England taught the Americans all they have of speech, or thought, hitherto. What thoughts they have not learned from England are foolish thoughts; what words they have not learned from England, unseemly words; the vile among them not being able to be humorous parrots, but only obscene mocking birds.[16]

As time passes, and as we in this country display more interest in and intelligence about our particular kind of English it will become increasingly clear that etymologies that will do very well for explaining how English people acquired their words will not do at all as explanations of how we in this country acquired the same words.

Unfortunately, up to the present time general dictionaries have been unable to point out in an appropriate manner the place of origin of the large number of quite respectable contributions we have made in this country to the English vocabulary. At the same time, dictionaries are often able to indicate what may be called "areas of usage," and it is helpful to have them perform this appropriate service. But when our dictionaries indicate, quite properly, that such words as *bozo* and *hobo* are confined to United States usage, and fail to credit us with having contributed to the language such useful words as *appendicitis, hydrant, urinalysis*, and many more, the over-all effect is to minister to the feeling that 'bad' words are American and good words are not.

Of course, as time passes on, and as scholars become more and more informed about the contributions made in this country to the resources of the language, dictionaries will undoubtedly be both able and willing to give us deserved credit for the enrichments we have made to the common language. A welcome indication of how quick lexicographers are to avail themselves of such etymological information as is now gradually being supplied them about words of American origin is seen in the care they now take to point out the American provenience of certain meanings of such words as *billion, campus, consular flag, creek, flat top,* and many others.

At a later time, they will be careful no doubt to call attention to such a word as *gumbo* as having originated in this country, having here been taken over from the language of slaves. Those who brought the word to our shores may well have come from the Belgian Congo, or from Angola, for in these regions in Africa this word is used in the sense of okra. Unlike the borrowings so far discussed from the African languages, *gumbo* has not only developed several meanings among us, but has entered into compounds such as *gumbo soup* and others now no longer used, as *gumbo ball, gumbo file, gumbo okra, gumbo French,* etc.

The plant name *benne* is a word of especial interest to philologists. The first time *benne* appeared in an English dictionary, so far as I have discovered, was in 1828 when it was included in the first of the long series of Webster's unabridged works. In the 1828 edition *benne* did not get in as a separate entry, but it occurs under the entry *Sesame, Sesamum* where with reference to this plant the statement is made: "One species of it is cultivated in Carolina, and the blacks use the seeds for food. It is called there *bene.*" In the next edition of Webster, that of 1841, *bene* was entered in its proper alphabetical place as has been done ever since, but in one of the early editions, perhaps first in that of 1864, the word was provided with an etymology which derived it from Malay. Somewhat incongruously in this same edition of Webster the word was defined as follows: "The *sesamus orientale,* or oil plant, of the West Indies, from the seeds of which an oil is expressed called benne-oil, used in medicine as a laxative."

Who the gentleman was who ventured to derive *benne* from Malay will probably never be known. I have a suspicion that it might well have been Dr. C. A. F. Mahn, Professor of Philology at the University of Berlin, but I am unable to prove that he was the culprit. Anyway, this error has persisted in all subsequent editions of Webster's dictionary, though in the current edition the plant in question is no longer associated with the West Indies. In the *Century Dictionary* of 1889 both the plant and its name were associated with the same part of the world, the word being still derived from Malay, but the plant being referred to India and adjacent regions.

There is nothing any clearer than that the word *benne* passed into the English language first here in the South,[17] and that it did so as a direct taking over from African slaves of a word they brought with them from Africa where they had made the acquaintance of the plant before they were brought to this country. Bernard Romans, a British traveler writing of Florida in 1775 reported, speaking of this plant, "The negroes use it as food either raw, toasted, or boiled in their soups and are fond of it; they call it Benni." We have already called attention to the fact that in 1828 Webster reported that the word used in Carolina for the plant was *bene,* and that the plant was cultivated there, the blacks using the seeds as food.

The fame of the cooking of the old time southern mammies has become a tradition which constitutes the background of the present pre-eminent reputation that southern cooks enjoy. It is not surprising therefore that some African words having to do with food have become part of our southern vocabulary, although on the colloquial level.

Formerly in the French quarter of New Orleans there was sold by Creole and Negro women a sweetened rice cake called a *cala* suitable for serving with coffee. Dr. Turner found that the African word *kala,* meaning rice, still survives in the language of the Gullah Negroes, and he also found unmistakable evidence that the word stems from Africa, Liberia, and Sierra Leone being regions from which the early slaves might have come who brought this word with them.

Webster's dictionary records *jambalaya* and defines it as rice and meat, usually ham, cooked together. The dictionary should perhaps have specified that the term is a local one, being used, so far as I know, only in the New Orleans area. The dish which it names is a Spanish-Creole one made with rice and some other ingredient, as chicken, turkey, sausage, crabs, etc.

The word itself has not been satisfactorily etymologized. Webster suggests that it may be a Negro corruption of the French word *jambon* meaning 'ham.' But there is a possibility that the Congo *chimbolo, zimbolo,* bread, biscuit, may be the source of the New Orleans *jambalaya.*

In that part of the *Century Dictionary* which came out in 1889 there occurs the word *foo-foo* and the definition given of it is: "A negro name for dough made from plantains, the fruit being boiled and then pounded in a mortar." The use of this word in the *Century* is the only evidence of its existence, so there is not much likelihood that its currency is very widespread.

However, there is in Gullah a word *fufu,* meaning mush, wheat flour made into a thin batter and cooked. In the Ewe speech used in Togo and Dahomey the same term occurs, used in the sense of yam, cassava, and coco boiled and pounded. The same term occurs in Senegal and Gambia and in Dahomey in the sense, usually, of food made from corn. The word exists in other African languages as well, but these are sufficient to indicate quite clearly the source of the word in American English. Like the others we are here dealing with, it is derived from the African slaves formerly among us.

It is a great mistake to regard the large unabridged dictionaries as containing all the words in the language. The fact is that there are approximately as many words in use that are not in the dictionary as are to be found in those compilations. For the purpose of calling attention to and emphasizing this fact I am including here a word which, so far as I know, has rarely appeared in print. The likelihood is that very few people even know that it ever existed. My father, who was born in south central Alabama in 1852, and who grew up under slavery conditions and in constant association with Negroes, sometimes used the expression *gunger bread* to refer to a delicious kind of molasses cake perhaps two or more inches thick usually baked in a square or rectangular pan.

I am sorry that I never asked my father where he got this name. As a boy I wondered somewhat vaguely if *gunger* and *conjure* were related, and if *gunger bread* was the kind to *conjure* with. So far as I was concerned, it would have been a most potent means for that purpose. When I grew older I wondered if *gunger bread* could be a playful mispronunciation of *ginger bread*. This may be the source of it, but I am inclined to think that the expression was another one, like *cooter,* which drifted into my father's speech from the lingo of his colored associates, because to this day the Gullah Negroes speak of molasses bread as *kanjabread,* or *kanja,* which is really 'ginger bread,' *kanja* or *ganga,* in their speech, and in that of the natives of northern Nigeria, being the word for ginger.

The word *cush* for us Southerners of an earlier generation stirs fond recollections of a dish which in my boyhood was regarded as the ne plus ultra of the culinary art. It has not received at the hands of lexicographers and philologists the careful attention which it richly deserves. In the Old South it was the word used for what in these far more degenerate days is known as *dressing,* that is, the breaded preparation placed inside and about a chicken when baked. I have in these later years bowed to the inevitable and refer, on those rare occasions when kind fate permits me to encounter this rare treat, the more conventional word *dressing* but deep down inside of me I know that the soul-stirring, stomach-filling material when properly prepared is in reality *cush.* Sometimes my aesthetic senses are offended by hearing this delicious food referred to as *stuffin,* a term which in this connection should be outlawed by Congressional enactment.

As I have indicated, the word has not been well treated in the dictionaries. Webster has it, with no indication of its source, and with very little indication that the authorities who compiled that work knew what the word means. The definition given is "Bread or crackers boiled and seasoned, as in water in which meat has been cooked." I should think that one dose of such a lugubrious preparation as this would be the end, and a most horrible end at that, of anyone forced to swallow it. *Cush* as I knew it was prepared from the meal of Indian corn, worked into a thick dough into which chopped up onions, pepper and salt, and perhaps other enticing ingredients that I was not aware of, were suitably interspersed. And in all cases this preparation was baked thoroughly in immediate or quite close contact with a chicken intended by nature and by the laws of health and sanitation to be partaken of as food by human beings. It was not to be wasted on one of those poor, emaciated, heartbroken things found dead around the place somewhere and sent off to the city as a good riddance and pounced upon there by ignorant people on the verge of starvation. One of the characteristics, however, of this word *cush* is that it is applied variously, so perhaps too much emphasis should not be placed upon the rather disappointing job done on the definition in the latest Webster.

It affords me great pleasure to be the first individual, so far as I know, ever to trace out, briefly, the path by which this word entered the speech of Southerners.

In the earliest, 1770, evidence we have of the word in use in this country, it occurs in the form *cushie,* meaning a kind of pancake made of Indian meal. This first example of the word comes from Maryland, in a region not a great ways from Annapolis. The ending *-ie,* justifies the suspicion that the immediate source of *cushie* might have been Dutch. Certainly the word *cush* passed into Dutch, where it is spelled *koeskoes.* Fortunately there is an etymological dictionary of the Dutch language, and by reference to that scholarly work we find that *koeskoes* is a Dutch borrowing from the French *couscous.*

There are, again fortunately, excellent etymological dictionaries of the French language, and when we turn to one of these we are informed that the French word *couscous* is not a native French word but has been taken into that language from the language of the Arabs. A fair sprinkling of Arabian words has passed into French, and this term happens to be one of them. As it was used by the Arabs, it meant flour slightly aspersed with water which by force of being stirred forms itself into little grains about like the head of a pin. It was prepared with meat and butter somewhat like rice. It is surprising, therefore, that the definition given in the Dutch dictionary of *koeskoes* is "A mixture of different kinds of meat, greens, etc."

The date at which Dutchmen borrowed this word of theirs from the French I find nowhere specified, but no matter when that borrowing took place, the Dutch in this country were in no wise dependent on the French for this word. They could have borrowed it, just as we did, from the Africans whom the Dutch, no less than our ancestors, were accustomed to hold in bondage. Turner records that in Gullah the term *cush,* and also the fuller form *cushcush,* occur in the sense of cornmeal dough sweetened and fried. This meaning of the term reminds us strongly of that meaning of *cushie* we have already noticed prevailing in Maryland about 1770, namely a kind of pancake made of Indian corn.

The evidence submitted by Dr. Turner makes it conclusive that the Gullahs have preserved over here a word which their ancestors brought out of Africa with them, for in northern Nigeria and in Angola as well this term *kushkush* prevails. In some of the dialects it is used of a thin cake made of ground-nuts, but in others it means a wheaten food, or parched meal.

With the information supplied by Dr. Turner the whole story of *cush* stands revealed. The word was not native with the Africans. It was one of the many words that have at one time or another passed from the Arabian language into one or another of the Af-

rican dialects. From Africa the word was trans-
mitted widely. In this country the slaves were not
only hewers of wood and drawers of waters; they
were cookers of food as well. It is not to be wondered at that this perfectly good Arabian word, *cush*
or *kushkush,* was made use of by the old slave mammies nor is it anything other than likely that they
fed what they called *cush* to the great men of the
South about as soon as they arrived on this earth
and had sufficiently oriented themselves to be able
to sit up and demand nourishment. Along with the
food these children probably imbibed the name for
it, and thus *cush* found early and satisfactory use
both in nourishing the "white folks" and in enrich-
ing their vocabulary. It is a great pity that the word
is not in more widespread use.

In concluding this discussion of African contributions to the plantation vocabulary, we should of
course point out that there were numerous terms
that can not be fitted into any of the categories already set up. Limitations of space, however, will
prevent us from discussing many of these.

We have already noticed in discussing *cush* that
with regard to some of the terms the slaves brought
us, they acted as carriers of words that were not,
to begin with, of African ancestry. The sad lot of
the slaves caused them to take up perforce words

from many sources and scatter them wherever it was their fate to be carried. Negroes serving Spanish, Portuguese, Dutch, and French masters had to learn enough of these languages to get along with, and then when the fortunes of their servitude changed and they came under the rulership of English-speaking masters they might well transmit to their new owners words they had picked up from non-English-speaking Europeans.

This process took place in the case of the word *pickaninny*. It originated out of an attempt by Negroes in the West Indies to pronounce some such expression as the Portuguese *pequenino* meaning very little or tiny, or the Spanish *pequeño niño*, little boy. No matter what the exact ingredients were that went into the make-up of *pickaninny*, the term itself spread widely, being carried into all parts of the world by Europeans as well as by Negroes. The word got into southern and central African use, probably carried thither by the English, or possibly by the Dutch, into whose language it passed in Dutch Guinea in South America. In Africa it is applied to the children of Kaffirs, Mashonas, etc. The English took it to Australia and used it of the children of the aborigines. And some of the natives there took the word over into their own speech. Slaves, no doubt those who had seen service in the West Indies.

brought the word into the United States, where, as
we all know, it is a common designation for a Negro
child. Quite clearly, the dissemination of words occasioned by slavery is something which the student
of language has to take into account.[18]

Some of those who know very little else about
Southern speech are aware of our use of *tote* in the
sense of to carry. A good many heads have been
bothered, and many pens set to work, in an effort to
account for this common southern colloquial expression. Now that Doctor Turner has completed his
study of Gullah, there is no longer any reason for
failing to recognize that this term is an Africanism
brought to this country early in the seventeenth century and in use here ever since. The Gullahs still use
it, and the indications are clear that in doing so they
are carrying on a linguistic usage brought over from
Africa. The word occurs in Angola and in the Belgian Congo meaning 'to pick up.' In the Ewe language of the Togo and Dahomey regions what is es-
sentially the same word means to lift a load from
one's head without help. In the Kimbundu and Um-
bundu languages *tuta* means to carry.

Our information is much better now than it was
when the editors of the *Oxford English Dictionary*,
in dealing with *tote* wrote a small type note beginning: "For an alleged Negro origin there is no foun-

dation." Doctor Turner has supplied a foundation that will not easily be removed.

In conclusion I wish to direct attention to a word that is of only local use, but which nevertheless possesses great linguistic interest. It occurs chiefly in the Brunswick and St. Simon's Island area of Georgia, an area which is extremely rich in historical and romantic lore. For example, on the north end of St. Simon's Island Aaron Burr stayed for a time in the summer of 1804 when New York and New Jersey were debating the question of which of them should deal with him for having killed Alexander Hamilton in a duel. The house in which he lived and from which he wrote letters to his beloved daughter Theodosia, was once palatial, but is now in ruins. It, and many others in that region where there formerly lived wealthy and cultured people, was made of what is called *tabby*, and it is this word which we now proceed to discuss.

When *tabby* was being edited for the *Oxford English Dictionary* the editors had at their disposal some examples that did not fit into the picture presented by the other uses of the word. The conventional word *tabby,* used originally of a kind of silk taffeta, is of Arabian origin and preserves the name of that quarter of Bagdad in which this material was made in early times. The word came into the English language in the seventeenth century, and developed several additional meanings, the one having reference to a tabby cat being now perhaps the best known.

As has been said, the editors of the *Oxford English Dictionary* had at their disposal some examples of a word *tabby* that had reference to a "concrete formed of a mixture of lime with shells, gravel, or stones in equal proportions, which when dry becomes very hard." The editors were not able to see how a word so radically different in meaning from that having reference to silken material could stem from the same source, and they expressed their inability to see how such a sense could have arisen.

Although the editors of the *Oxford English Dictionary* do not appear to have realized it, the earliest evidence for *tabby* in this sense of a kind of concrete is American in origin. The fact is that the slaves who were brought into that part of Georgia along the coast where this word *tabby* is still used brought the word with them from Africa. At the present time the Gullahs speak of a *tabi house* meaning a house made of cement and oyster shells with which pieces of brick are frequently mixed. Those Gullahs who now use this word *tabby* are preserving in their speech a word which their ancestors brought from the Dark Continent. *Tabby* however is not a word of African origin, but is one of the many Arabic words that have passed into one or another of the African languages. Consequently our friends in Georgia who use this word *tabby* are in reality speaking Arabic without perhaps suspecting it.[19]

Notes

1. The feeling is growing on the part of students of language that the older, traditional studies in "Germanic Philology" are losing their interest because the field has been pretty well exhausted by the research done during the past half century. No really big challenging things remain. Undoubtedly the modern fields are now gaining in importance and attention.

2. See Arthur E. Morgan, *Nowhere Was Somewhere* (Chapel Hill, 1946), 187 ff.

3. The literature on the origin of the American Indians is of course most voluminous. One of the latest books on the subject is that by Paul S. Martin, George I. Quimby, and Donald Collier, *Indians Before Columbus/Twenty Thousand Years of North American History Revealed by Archaeology* (Chicago, 1947). Another excellent but slightly older work is Diamond Jenness, ed., *The American Aborigines/Their Origin and Antiquities* (Toronto, 1933). Shorter treatments may be found in encyclopedias. Archaeologists are busy in the Valley of Mexico, as elsewhere. See *Newsweek,* April 21, 1947, 61, for an account of the finding on February 22 of this year of "the oldest dated remains of man in the Americas." This find, near Tepexpan, a few miles north of Mexico City, is thought to be 15,000 years old, but the Tepexpan man must have looked very much like a modern Indian.

4. The most outstanding work in this field is the *Handbook of American Indian Languages* by Franz Boas, which appeared in 1911 as Bulletin 40 (Pt. 1) of the U. S. Bureau of American Ethnology.

5. The literature on the Nahuatl Indians and their language is abundant. Good starting points are the *Encyclopedia Britannica* and the work of Jenness, already mentioned.

6. A full account of papermaking among these Indians is given in Victor Wolfgang Von Hagen, *The Aztec and Maya Papermakers* (New York, 1943). The author also has much to say about the pictographs produced by the Aztecs.

7. The most notable collection of reproductions of Aztec pictographs is that by Lord Kingsborough (1795-1837). As a young man, the Earl of Kingsborough traveled much in Mexico, became deeply interested in the antiquities of that country and resolved to devote his life to a noble illustrated edition of these. He spent his life and his fortune on this task. When he had exhausted his resources, he was sued by a paper-maker, and confined in Marshalsea, where he contracted a malignant fever from which he died in a few weeks. Had he lived a few months longer he would have become the Earl of Kingston, and have received a stipend of forty thousand pounds a year. His work, in nine volumes, was printed in imperial folio, and included 1000 plates. Originally it sold for one hundred and forty pounds.

8. The name *Mexico* is connected with the name of the group of American tribes calling themselves *Mexica* (in the singular *Mexicatl*) or *Azteca*. The name of the national war-god to which the word is related or from which it is derived is *Mexitl,* or, more commonly, *Huitzilopochtli.* See *Ency. Brit.*

9. *Ency. Brit.* s.v. Aztec.

10. This explanation of *Nahuatl* I have encountered only once and that in the introduction of T. S. Denison, *Nauatl or Mexican in Aryan Phonology* (Chicago, 1907), a work which undertakes, quite unsuccessfully, to relate Nahuatl and Sanskrit.

11. *Ency. Brit.* s.v. Mexico.

12. C. A. Robelo, *Diccionario de aztequismos* (Cuernavaca, Mexico, 1904), 85. The Aztec word meaning locust or grasshopper, *chapul,* and the word for hill, *tepetl,* both passed into American Spanish, *chapulin* being a synonym for *langosta,* and *tepetl* appearing in numerous American Spanish compounds. See Francisco J. Santamaría, *Diccionario General de Americanismos* (Méjico, D. F., 1942).

Many Aztec pictographs of places the names of which end in *-epec* or *-tepec* make use of a hill with various animals and things on it. The final *-c* in such names has the force of *on,* so *Chapultepec,* as the Aztecs pictured it had the force of 'on the grasshopper hill.' See plates 2, 3, 7, 8, 12, 14, 15, 16, 17, 18, in Kingsborough.

13. *Cent. Dict. of Names.*

14. These discussions of words that came early into English and that were, in some cases, borrowed again in our Southwestern area, are based chiefly on such lexicographical evidence as that afforded by the *Oxford English Dictionary* and *Dictionary of American English,* as well as upon the works of Santamaría, Webster, and the Century.

15. Santamaría.

16. This change in the form of such a word as *Xalapa* into *Jalapa* reflects a shift in pronunciation. In the sixteenth century the Spanish used *x* for the *sh* sound we are familiar

with in such words as *shall, sure,* and many others. In time this palatal continuant in Spanish came to be made much further back in the mouth and the resulting sound, represented now by *j,* is that heard in the Spanish pronunciation of such words as *jalap* and *Mexico.* This sound shift will be referred to again in discussing *shack.*

17. George R. Stewart, *Names on the Land* (New York, 1945), 254. In addition to mentioning Chapultepec, Stewart lists also Monterey, Buena Vista, Palo Alto, Cerro Gorda, and Resaca as Mexican place names brought back by soldiers returning from the Mexican War. For the information about Jalapa, Ind., I am indebted to W. L. McAtee.

18. The reborrowing in this country of words that had earlier passed into the English of England had ramifications far too extensive to be gone into here. Many Spanish words, like *alcalde,* and *burro,* with no Aztec antecedents, have in their time entered the English language twice. And the same thing has been done by other words from such sources as German, Dutch, and French. Other Nahuatl words which, in my opinion, might be added to the list given here are *nopal, teocalli, zopilote.* There are no doubt others not so far suspected. Students hardly need to be reminded that borrowings from French at different times, or from different areas, have resulted in the appearance of closely related words as *ward, guard; wage, gage; wallop, gallop; gaol, jail,* etc. These phenomena, however, are entirely outside the scope of this study.

19. An excellent paper on the subject of Nahuatl words in American English was written by George Watson and appeared in *American Speech,* April 1938, pp. 108-21. I have used this study freely in my discussions of individual terms.

In the preparation of his paper, Watson leaned heavily upon "A Contribution Towards a Vocabulary of Spanish and Mexican Words Used in Texas," by H. Tallichet which appeared in *Dialect Notes* I. 185ff.

20. Santamaría.

21. Watson, p. 116.

22. This disagreement exists between Santamaría and Frederick Webb Hodge, ed. *Handbook of American Indians North of Mexico . . . in Two Parts* (Washington, 1907, 1910), II, 237. The article on *peyote* in Hodge was written by James Mooney of the Bureau of American Ethnology. In addition to deriving the word from Nahuatl *peyotl,* 'caterpillar,' referring to the downy center of the button, Mooney gives some account of the place occupied by the peyote in the life and customs of the Indians. The etymology in Hodge was taken over into Webster's dictionary. Santamaría, on the other hand, explains the Nahuatl word as meaning 'that which deceives or gives valor to,' and gives an interesting account of some of the uses made of the plant by the Indians.

23. See the *Dictionary of American English* s.v. Jamestown weed.

24. Dr. Francis made the following statement about his originating this name. It is found in the 1921 *Public Health Reports,* 29 July, p. 1731n: "The name tularæmia is based on the specific name *Bacterium tularense,* plus *æmia,* from the Greek, and has reference to the presence of this bacterium in the blood, on the analogy of leukæmia or bacteræmia, etc. The names thus far used for this disease are strictly vernacular and do not lend themselves to international usage as easily as a name in Latin form."

25. Other Nahuatl borrowings, most of them plant

names, are: *amole, ayacahuita pine, bisnaga, cacomite, camote, canatilla, capules, capulin, chacate, chicalote, chilaquiles, chiltapin, chapote, huajillo, huisache, jicama, ocote, ocotillo, sacate, sacaton, sapota, sotol, teocote, tepejilote, tequesquite, tequila.*

26. The Aztec *claco* was taken up into Mexican Spanish and thence into American English, and used as the name of a small coin worth about three cents formerly current in Mexico and the Southwest. See Santamaría and *Dictionary of American English.*

27. I am indebted to W. L. McAtee for this information.

28. Santamaría has a full account of the word.

CHAPTER 2 • SOME MUSKHOGEAN WORDS IN THE SOUTHERN VOCABULARY

1. *U. S. Bureau of Ethnology 7th Ann. Rept.* (Washington, 1891), 95. There is a map showing the areas occupied by various linguistic families of American Indians in this work. This map is also found in the back of volume I of Hodge, *Handbook of American Indians.*

2. Thomas M. Owen, *History of Alabama and Dictionary of Alabama Biography* (Chicago, 1921) II, 1242ff.

3. Frederick W. Hodge, ed., *Handbook of American Indians,* s.v. Muskhogean Family.

4. Hodge favors the usual view that the number of streams in their country accounts for the name *Creeks* given them by white settlers. W. A. Read, *Florida Place-Names of Indian Origin* (Baton Rouge, 1934), 61, thinks the name was probably shortened from "Ocheese Creek Indians,"

Ocheese, he says, "being the name of a stream on which most of the so-called Lower Creeks at one time were living."

5. Hodge s.v. Apalachicola says the word possibly means 'people on the other side.' Professor Wyman, as shown on page 83, interprets the name as meaning 'helping people, allies.' W. A. Read in his *Indian Place-Names in Alabama* (Baton Rouge, 1937), 5, makes no mention of Wyman's explanation, but agrees with Hodge. Dr. John R. Swanton of the Bureau of American Ethnology, Smithsonian Institution, in a review which he wrote of Dr. Read's work (see *American Speech,* 1937, pp. 212-15), without mentioning Dr. Wyman's explanation, favors the view which he expressed.

6. W. A. Read, *Louisiana Place-Names of Indian Origin* (Baton Rouge, 1927), 22. Swanton, *loc. cit.* says: "While this word [Chickasaw] cannot be translated, it seems probable that the ending is the common Choctaw and Chickasaw locative ending -asha, 'it sits there,' or 'it is there.' "

7. Halbert thought the name *Choctaw* might signify "separation." See Read, *Louisiana Place-Names,* 24. Hodge mentions the possibility of *Choctaw* being related to the Spanish *chato,* which, on purely linguistic grounds, is entirely possible.

8. Scholars are agreed on this interpretation of *Seminole.* See Hodge and Read.

9. See note 1 above.

10. Franz Boas in his *Handbook of American Indian Languages* Part I (Washington, 1911), 82-3 lists 55 linguistic families in North America north of Mexico. In the *Sixth Report of the U. S. Geographic Board* (Washington,

1932), 12-13, the number is placed at 45, with a grand total of more than 650 dialects.

11. James C. Pilling, *Bibliography of the Muskhogean Languages* (Washington, 1889), 16-17.

12. Owen, III, 723-4.

13. Pilling, 57.

14. Boas, 74 ff., Hodge, s.v. Languages. Silas T. Rand in *Micmac Dictionary* (Charlottetown, P.E.I., 1902) on p. xii, with reference to the polysynthetic character of Micmac, mentions a Micmac word meaning "I hear him singing in the distance though I do not see him."

15. Swanton, *loc. cit.*: "C. A. Hanna (*The Wilderness Trail,* p. 215) seems to have shown that this was the Iroquois name for the Shawnee town known as Eskippakithiki on the Indian Old Fields in Clark County, Kentucky, or at least the name of the prairie surrounding it."

16. *Sixth Rept. of the U. S. Geographic Board,* 14. Also Francis W. Halsey, *A Tour of Four Great Rivers* (New York, 1906) liii. The difficulty of recognizing and recovering the significance of Indian names is very great and has been well dealt with. Boas, p. 62, says: "The translations of Indian names which are popularly known—like Sitting-Bull, Afraid-Of-His-Horse, etc.—indicate that names possess a deeper significance. The translations, however, are so difficult that a thorough linguistic knowledge is required in order to explain the significance adequately."

17. Alexander B. Meek had a brother, Benjamin Franklin Meek who taught English at the University of Alabama from 1871 till his death in 1899.

18. The interpretations of this and subsequently men-

tioned Indian names are taken from the excellent studies already mentioned of Doctor W. A. Read of Louisiana State University. In the case of many of the names, Hodge also has been consulted with profit.

19. The Alabama state seal bearing the "Here We Rest" motto was the result of contemptible Reconstruction skulduggery. The carpetbagger legislature of 1868 abolished the original state seal, substituting one consisting of the shield of the U. S. seal—not a palatable emblem in the defeated South just at that time—on which an American eagle was represented bearing in his beak a scroll on which "Here We Rest" appeared. Seventy-one years later, the Alabama legislature of 1939, without a dissenting vote, got round to doing away with this vestige of evil days by restoring the original state seal designed in 1817 before the coming on the scene of that imaginative Alabama author who dreamed up the "Here We Rest" tale. See the pamphlet *Alabama State Emblems* distributed by Alabama State Department of Archives and History, at Montgomery.

20. The Smithsonian Institution got out a mimeographed release for Sunday, July 25, 1937, in which the view is expressed that *Alabama* is from the Choctaw words *alba,* vegetation and *amo,* to cut or gather. Dr. John R. Swanton, in his review of Dr. Read's *Indian Place-Names in Alabama,* commented as follows on *Alabama.* " 'Here we rest' is, of course definitely 'out' as an interpretation of this name. Originally it probably belonged to a single town. The interpretation Professor Read gives is valid but inasmuch as all of the Southeastern Indians were 'thicket clearers,' I have thought that reference might be had to medicines, the town having been noted for its medicine men or its proximity to

quantities of medicine plants. In that case we must suppose alba to be understood in an esoteric sense just as the Creek word for 'leaf' came to be applied to the *Ilex vomitoria*." See *Amer. Speech*, 1937, 212-13.

21. Hodge and Read devote attention to this name. See also *Sixth Report of the U. S. Geographic Board*, 14.

22. Smithsonian Release (see note 20.)

23. In his work on the Byington dictionary, *s.v. moeli*, Halbert wrote the following note: "As a plural verb of action it means not only to skim, but to row, to paddle, to scull; it is used to denote the paddling of boats or canoes. There is reason to believe that in this word we have the tribal name, Maubila or Mauilla. Mobile is called by the modern Choctaw Moilla, a form resembling both *moeli* and Mauilla."

24. Read in his book on Florida place-names, 78-9, discusses the prosaic quality of Indian names. (See note 26 below.) Professor Read in his *Indian Place-Names in Alabama*, after giving the literal interpretation of *Notasulga*, 'many teeth,' points out: "The Creek term for the angelica (genus *Ammiaceæ*) is *notosa;* and a group of plants of this species would be called *notosalgi,* a compound of *notosa* and the collective suffix *algi*." Dr. Swanton in his review of Read favors this derivation from the name of the angelica, and agrees that the plant name is derived from the expression meaning 'many teeth.'

25. See Read, *Indian Place-Names in Alabama,* and Swanton, *loc. cit.,* s.v. Talladega.

26. Halbert in *Trans. Ala. Hist. Soc.* II, 108 discusses in some detail Pushmataha's name. The Choctaws in ordinary conversation elided many of their vowels and consonants. The full name of this chief was something like *Apush imalhtaha,*

which results from *Apushi im alhtaha,* 'the sapling is ready or finished for him,' a name probably given in babyhood for some trivial and soon forgotten reason. Halbert regards as not worthy of serious consideration Brewer's interpretation of Pushmataha's name as meaning 'he has won all the honors of his race.'

I am fortunately able to add here another interpretation of this renowned warrior's name which has just reached me in an irate communication from Mrs. R. H. Thompson, Birmingham, Michigan, a lady of Indian descent who takes me severely to task for having in this lecture which she had read about in her home town paper referred to Indians as prosaic. She interprets Pushmataha's name as meaning in Choctaw 'His arm, and weapons in his hand, are fatal to his foe.' I take pleasure in here retracting my statement about Indian prosaicness so far as Mrs. Thompson and Pushmataha are concerned.

27. In World War II some of our paratroopers used *Osceola!* as a battle cry. See Keith Ayling, *They Fly to Fight* (New York, 1944). *Osceola* is sometimes used as a name for a girl.

28. The Byington Choctaw dictionary is provided with an English-Choctaw index, enabling the user of it to find readily the terms used by the Choctaws for a large number of English words.

29. W. R. Gerard wrote an interesting account of plant names of Indian origin which appeared in *Garden & Forest,* June 24, July 1, 15, 22, 29, 1896. Much of what is here said about plant names from the Muskhogean dialects comes from these articles, but Hodge has also supplied considerable information.

30. Southern fishermen use, when they can get them, catawba worms, found on the leaves of the catawba or catalpa in the early summer, and regarded as superior fish bait.

31. At the close of this lecture I was properly humbled by having an esteemed and cultured friend who was brought up near Bayou Labatre tell me that she had never heard any other pronunciation than *Bilerbatry!*

CHAPTER 3 • AFRICANISMS IN THE PLANTATION VOCABULARY

1. See the *Oxford English Dictionary.*

2. In these opening paragraphs I have drawn on Elizabeth Donnan, *Documents Illustrative of the Slave Trade to America,* 4 vols. (1930-35). The fourth volume, devoted to "The Border Colonies and the Southern Colonies," has many tables showing the number of Negroes imported into Maryland, Virginia, South Carolina, Georgia and Louisiana. These lists give the names and owners of the slave ships, the number and source of the slaves in each shipment, and more statistical data.

Another work which I have found useful is Frederick Bancroft, *Slave Trading in the Old South* (Baltimore, 1931).

3. *Gullah* is of course a Southernism of African origin. It may be a shortening of *Angola,* or from the name of a Liberian tribe and its language.

4. See *Dictionary of American English* s.v. Obeah.

5. M. S. De Vere, *Americanisms* 138.

6. In dealing with this and the following terms, I have drawn heavily on the Turner MS., and on dictionaries, esp. the *Dictionary of American English.*

7. See W. A. Read, *La.-French* (1931) s.v. calinda.

8. H. Harrower, *Diary* 93.

9. J. F. D. Smyth, *Tour in the U. S.* (London, 1784) I, 46.

10. This excerpt is from the collectanea of Albert Matthews of Boston. His source was *A New History of Jamaica* published in London in 1740.

11. See the *Oxford English Dictionary* s.v. Banjo.

12. See the *Dictionary of American English* s.v. Banjor. A. W. Read has pointed out in his article in *Dialect Notes* for Dec. 1933, p. 358 that Boucher may have taken over at least some of the words he included in his "Pastoral" from reading books about the West Indies, and therefore may not have been recording the speech of the people about him in Maryland. This point is well taken. James Grainger, in his work on sugar-cane Bk. iv. 584*n* explains "banshaw" as meaning "a sort of rude guitar, invented by the Negroes. It produces a wild pleasing melancholy sound." His observations were made on St. Christopher's Island, in the West Indies. The fact is worth noticing that Santamaría records *banjo* in his dictionary of Americanismos, and defines it as follows: Instrumento músico de cuerda, parecido a la guitarra, propio de los negros y creado por ellos. Hoy se usa en la música social europea y americana. Es instrumento de pocas variaciones.

Harry R. Warfel in his book on Noah Webster (1936), p. 292 lists several of the jibes directed at Webster belittling his intentions of making an American dictionary. One of these was as follows: "Massa Webster plese put sum Hommany and sum Good Possum fat and sum two tree good

Banjoe in your new what-you-call-um Book for your fello
Cytzen [signed] Cuffee."

13. F. Moore, *Voyage to Ga.* (1744) 57, in Ga. Hist.
Soc. *Collections* I.

14. *Southern Tour* II, 102.

15. *Sugar-Cane* Bk. IV, 275n. The insect described in
the passage given is the flea which dictionaries call a *chigoe*.
Our southern *chigger* or *red bug* is often confused with this
chigoe. Our insect is also sometimes known as a *jigger*.

16. *Fors Clavigera* xlii, 118.

17. The earliest evidence I have found for the word
benne is in the *Amer. Philos. Soc.* I, 309. John Morel of Savannah, Ga., writing in 1769, said: "I send you a small keg
of Bene or Bene Seed, which you will please to present to
your Society for their inspection." Morel suggested the possibility of cultivating the plant as far north as Philadelphia,
as a source of table oil, the report being that 100 pounds of
the seed would yield 90 pounds of oil. Sheila Hibben, in her
American Regional Cookery (Boston, 1946) p. 316 gives a
recipe for making Charleston Benné Wafers. The recipe calls
for ½ cup of parched benne seeds. The form *benné* shows
that the author regarded the word as French.

I am informed by Dr. Isidore Dyen of Yale that in Malay
bijan, (Javanese *wijen*) is the word meaning sesame. It is a
far cry from such forms as *bijan, wijen* to *benne*. Dr. Dyen
tells me that there is a Malay word *bëneh,* 'seed,' but its resemblance to *benne* is undoubtedly accidental.

18. The passing of African words into various Indian
languages has, so far as I know, never been investigated.
Like many other Indians, the Seminoles owned slaves, and I

have come across three instances of African words passing into the speech of these Indians. In *Publications of the Alabama Historical Society* I, 396 there is listed "Fulemmy's Town, a Seminole settlement inhabited by Chiaha Indians; was also called Pinder-Town." There is a reference to this passage in John R. Swanton's *Early History of the Creek Indians,* (Washington, 1922) p. 407*n.,* and Swanton also makes a reference to Bucker Woman's Town on the Suwanee River. Both these place-names, "Pinder-Town" and "Bucker Woman's Town," involve African terms, "Bucker" being undoubtedly the same as "buckra" mentioned in note 19 below.

Also there is in *Niles' Register,* volume 57, 168-9, an account of how two soldiers accompanied by a Negro interpreter were sent on a mission to some Seminole Indians who had, in a time of supposed peace, invited some white officers to a dance. The two soldiers were killed and the interpreter barely saved his life by hiding in a river with only the tip of his nose above water. The Seminoles hunted for him, and passed so near him that he could hear them talking. Women took part in this hunt. "One of the laughing squaws remarked as she was passing, 'I think that interpreter is dead—for he fell sideways into the river as if he was wounded;' and appeared to be delighted at his fate—'he was so swongo' (proud) said she." Turner lists "swango" as in use among the Gullahs, and refers it back to Mende (Sierra Leone) in which language it means to be proud, evil, lascivious.

19. The Arabic *tabix,* cement, mortar, brick, passed, as did a very large number of Arabic words, into Spanish, and accounts for *tabicon,* an augmentative of *tabique,* a wall of brick.

In the present state of our investigations into the sources

of American English it is not possible to make out a complete
list of those words which have come into our variety of English from slaves. Some of those terms for which a positive,
or at least a good, case can now be made out are:

bozo See *American Speech* for April, 1939, p. 97.
    Turner cites this word used among the Gullahs as
    a name signifying great cheapness.

buckra (meaning a white man). This term has been rec-
    ognized as an Africanism for a long time.

congo W. A. Read in his *La.-French*, p. 121 lists this
    word as used in the New Orleans area for a moc-
    casin, or for a bluish-black eel-like amphibian.

doney *doney gal.* These expressions with reference to a
    girl are listed by Harold Wentworth in his *Dic-
    tionary of American Dialect.* Turner lists the Gul-
    lah feminine personal name *doni,* and refers it back
    to Bambara *doni,* a burden.

Ebo See the *Dictionary of American English.*

juba The *Dictionary of American English* lists this word
    in the sense of a Negro rollicking dance, but no
    satisfactory origin has been made out for it.

juke In recent years this term has come into wide use
    in the expression *juke-box.* Turner shows that it
    is unquestionably an Africanism, the word being
    common among the Gullahs in the sense of in-
    famous, disorderly, its most common use being in
    the combination *juke-house.* Webster gives it as
    of Southern origin. A very remarkable but quite
    unbelievable etymology for *juke* is given at some
    length in the *N. Y. Times Mag.* 14 April, 1946, p.

31. The statement is there made that the word is of old English ancestry, going back to *iowken,* to rest, sleep, which Chaucer used in "Troilus and Criseyde." This word was brought into the mountains of this country and preserved there in the form *jouke.* Since mountaineers were accustomed to foregather at taverns to rest and lounge, they began to call the tavern a 'jouke joint,' and when a music box was set up in such a place the instrument became a *jook box,* modern *juke box.* This etymology is of course of imagination all compact, except that there is in Chaucer's "Troilus" the word *iowken,* meaning to lie asleep or at rest. The *Oxford English Dictionary* s.v. Jouk v[1] shows that the word lasted till about 1400, and records a pseudo-archaic use in *a*1652.

lagniappe Webster etymologizes this word as made up of the French *la,* and the Spanish *ñapa, yapa.* Read in *La.-Fr.* agrees with this, but explains *ñapa* in the Spanish as being taken from Kechuan (a South American Indian language.) But Santamaría regards the base of the word as being of ultimate African, not South American, origin. See Santamaría, and *American Speech* XIV, 93-6, and *Zeitschrift für französische Sprache und Literatur* LXI, 77.

Index of words

cassina [kə'saɪnɑ] M 76
cassine [kə'sin] M 76
Catahoula [ˌkætə'hulə] M 68
catalpa [kə'tælpə] M 77
catawba [kə'tɔbə] M 77
Chacahoula [tʃæk'hulə; tʃakə-] M 68
chacate [tʃɑ'kate] N 135
chachalaca [ˌtʃatʃɑ'lakə] N 38
chapote [tʃɑ'pote] N 135
Chattahoochee [ˌtʃætə'hutʃɪ] M 57
chicalote [ˌtʃikalote] N 135
Chickasaw ['tʃɪkəˌsɔ] M 46, 136
chicle ['tʃɪkl̩] N 39
chigger ['tʃɪgə] A 107-110, 143
chilacayote [ˌtʃilakə'jotə] N 30
chilaquiles [ˌtʃilə'kwɪləz] N 135
chile colorado ['tʃɪlɪˌkalə'rædo; 'rado] N 18
chile con carne ['tʃɪlɪ'kan'ka(r)nɪ] N 18
chilicothe [ˌtʃɪlə'kaθɪ] N 30, 31
chilli ['tʃɪlɪ] N 17, 18
chiltepin [ˌtʃiltə'pin] N 135
Choctaw ['tʃaktɔ] M 47, 136
chumpa (girl) ['tʃʌmpə] M 81
claco ['klako] N 36
comal [ko'mal] N 39
Conecuh [kə'nekə] M 64, 68
congo ['kaŋgo] A 145
coontie ['kuntɪ] M 77
Coosa ['kusə] M 58
cooter ['kutə] M 92, 106-107, 119
coyote ['kaɪot; kaɪ'otɪ] N 37

Subject Index